MW00763897

Also from Second Wind Publishing
by Chuck Thurston

Senior Scribbles Unearthed

www.secondwindpublishing.com

Senior Scribbles
Second Dose

"Take Two of These
And Keep Your Mouth Shut"

By

Chuck Thurston

Running Angel Books
Published by Second Wind Publishing, LLC.
Kernersville

Running Angel Books
Second Wind Publishing, LLC
931-B South Main Street, Box 145
Kernersville, NC 27284

This book is not fiction. It is a collection of memoirs, observations, and stories concerning real people and events in most cases. Occasionally facts are embellished or situations are contrived to emphasize the absurdity of the situations described, but everything was prompted by actual events in the life of the author.

First Running Angel edition published December, 2013
Running Angel Books, Running Angel, and all production design are trademarks of Second Wind Publishing, used under license.

For information regarding bulk purchases of this book, digital purchase and special discounts, please contact the publisher at
www.secondwindpublishing.com

Cover design by Curt Thurston
Interior Illustrations by Grace Creed

Manufactured in the United States of America
ISBN 978-1-938101-91-5

To the Thurston Clan
—wherever and however they are

Acknowledgments

Yet again, I have to acknowledge my family, friends, acquaintances, casual and innocent passers-by, assorted critters and the other subjects and objects of my observation and contemplation—they have never failed to provide the inspiration, motivation, courage, cussedness, silliness, wisdom, insights and behaviors that are the grist for this second collection of Senior Scribbles.

And, once again, my special thanks to my son, Curt Thurston, for his great cover. He had to knock a little polish off his normal high tech computer generated graphics to give the old English grave robber another go around.

Look him up at curtthurston.com to see his day job stuff.

Another special thanks to Grace Creed, a wonderful artist, who accepted the challenge of providing the interior illustrations for this book on incredibly short notice. Grace never failed to come through – with work that speaks for her talent.

Her email is glceed@aol.com

INTRODUCTION

This is the second collection of Senior Scribbles—a worthy successor, I hope, to "Senior Scribbles Unearthed." A lesser man would be urging you to snap this up to join the first one on your shelf. A complete set of anything is always worth more than a single, isolated object. And though I wouldn't stoop to shameless hawking, I feel it's only fair to point out that I have almost enough material for a third book, and a set of three…well, you figure it out.

Many of these were first published in a small mountain newspaper in Brevard, North Carolina—*The Transylvania Times*. They are observations, reminiscences and (mostly) light hearted views of life, from one who has spent some time in it.

I might challenge a few pieces of conventional wisdom here and there, but I won't push any hardcore religious or philosophical stuff at you. You can get that from those funny TV stations with the high station numbers. My political views— common sense, I calls it—are obvious in a piece or two. If I can't say what's on my mind at *my* age—when can I, for heaven's sake?

If you like my stuff, drop me a line! If you don't—keep it to yourself!

—Chuck Thurston, Summer 2013

TABLE OF CONTENTS

FOOD, DRINKS AND HIJINKS

Feeding the Hungry

Primitive men and women were hunter-gatherers. Eating was catch as catch can. Sharing was essential. If one of them ran across a nut tree in the forest, he or she didn't keep it to himself or herself. Survival of their tribe demanded that the lucky forager run and tell the rest. They stored very little, but ate whatever could be consumed on the spot—and hunted for another source.

Some would say that the behavior of teenagers in the food court of a large mall suggests that this human instinct is still strong.

But in every age and in every way, humans periodically drop whatever else they are doing and hunt for chow.

My farm mother had five sons and a husband to deal with. We did grace on special occasions—large family gatherings, church holidays, etc., but my dad's everyday injunction, once the vittles were on the table, was to "grab and growl!"

Nothing was wasted.

Anything that survived our daily feedings went into the slop bucket for the hogs. It is certain that every now and then these critters dined on the remains of one of their comrades who had made the supreme sacrifice before them.

Were they sentient, they might have found some temporary solace in contemplating this cycle of nature. Temporary, I say—they were destined to be recycled into next winter's bacon.

There was a sign over the mess hall of one military installation I spent some time at. It read, "Take all you want, but eat all you take." I knew of guys who took this to heart. They would gobble down their first tray of food in a mad rush so they could get back in line for another go at it.

At one base, I was invited by one of the storekeepers to accompany him on a truck trip to a large depot that warehoused food meant for military installations in that particular section of the east coast. I was off duty and figured I would enjoy the ride. The SK had been given a list of items he was to pick up for our unit. They would be waiting to be loaded upon his arrival.

As he checked off his sheet, one of the warehouse workers informed him that there had been a run on the more popular ice cream flavors. All he had to give us was pistachio. We ate pistachio ice cream for the next several weeks. Look, most folks can breeze through a month with only chocolate or vanilla as their options. But pistachio? I have not touched it since.

My new wife could not cook—came from a long line of women who could not cook. I did not know this in advance. Actually she didn't either until she questioned her mother about *her* mother. She also questioned aunts, and various cousins…"Did you know that your great Aunt Agnette hated to cook?"

My wife dutifully passed this non-skill on to our daughter. As unluck would have it, our sons also married women who were happy to abandon the kitchen to their husbands. For all I know, this fear of the skillet and oven is being passed down to females yet unborn.

I knew a little, and was willing to experiment. I had to, really, for self-preservation. I became so familiar with Lipton's chicken noodle soup that I could tell when they made subtle changes to the formula. "Lipton's has done it again," I would say.

Early on she mastered eggs—boiled and scrambled, although an omelet escaped her—and does to this day.

When my wife and I raised a family of our own, we found out what generations of parents before us had already discovered.

Our boys had a garage rock band and the house was for some time a teen hangout. Rehearsals took place in our cellar game room. Other parents pointed out that we, at least, knew where they were. Oh, did we know. Every nail in the house was loose.

On one occasion, rehearsal coincided with our dinnertime,

and we had made a nice casserole. It wouldn't have fed them anyway, and a Matthew 14 loaves and fishes multiplication was beyond us. As the latest rock riffs billowed up from the basement and saturated the living quarters of the house, we called friends across town. Could we come to their place for dinner? We'd bring it! We put our casserole in the car and headed out.

No need for fine dining or niceties. Invariably our kids' pals would be guys from the swim or wrestling teams at the local high school. They were always in training. You have not lived until you have fed wrestlers who are moving up a weight class for a coming meet. We cooked spaghetti by the tub-full.

I used to do backpacking trips with my sons and an occasional buddy. On one such trip, we all packed one of the big chocolate mega bars...designed for a week's survival, I would guess. On the trail, I took mine out at occasional rest stops and nibbled a bite or two before putting it back in my pack. About an hour into the hike, the boys were eying my stash and confessed that they had polished off their own bars.

This particular trail bordered a vineyard in the New York grape country. It was no effort at all to hop off the trail a step or two and grab a bunch of grapes in passing. I am sure the vineyard owner planned on losing a few bunches to the occasional hikers. Luckily for him, the boys' plunder was limited to what they could carry in their hands without breaking stride on the hike. We grabbed an afternoon snack and trekked on.

That night we pulled into a family campground that was not far off our trail. I set up the tent, stowed the packs, lit a campfire, started the little gas stove to heat up some water—then relaxed while our freeze-dried food rehydrated for cooking.

After we had eaten, the boys wondered aloud if we might also finish off the breakfast stuff we had brought. And go hungry for breakfast? I couldn't believe this.

I pointed out that this was a family campground and there were probably lots of folks there with teenagers—likely a few girls, too. I assured them they weren't the worst looking boys in the state. Why not cruise the grounds, and casually, strike up a conversation here and there to see if a hotdog or burger invitation might be forthcoming?

Off they went. Hunters and—hopeful—gatherers.

For many years Jimmy Anderson ran a popular restaurant in Charlotte near the Presbyterian hospital. Jimmy was a genuine Greek—his son, Gary, told me his untranslated name would be Demostanis Anageros Andritsanos. I ate at Anderson's many times over the years, and never met Jimmy personally, but heard he was a genial and generous soul. He died in 1988 and many Charlotteans were saddened by the loss.

The restaurant picked up a lot of hospital traffic—patients and visitors coming and going. Some perhaps having a final restaurant meal before a hospital stay, or ones coming off a stay and back in the world of mashed potatoes, meatloaf, "The World's Best Pecan Pie," as Jimmy called it—and the other sturdy dishes that Jimmy served. It was not uncommon to see people with canes and crutches and bandages coming and going on the arm of caregivers. Uniformed nurses, doctors and local businessmen often complimented the crowd.

One day a woman with a small infant walked in—perhaps

in the neighborhood because of some hospital business. She asked Jimmy to give her a rear booth with a little privacy because she had to breast feed her baby. Jimmy graciously complied.

Although she was as discreet as she could possibly be, an observable customer noticed and complained to Jimmy. Jimmy replied, "Hey—everybody's gotta eat!"

Right on, Jimmy! RIP.

Portion Control

Everything seems to be getting smaller these days. Newspaper print has shrunk over the years and I can barely make out the buttons on my cell phone.

Just the other day I got the latest annual Sports Illustrated swimsuit issue. Oh, c'mon. Nothing in it qualifies as a swimsuit.

There is one area that is counter to this trend. Going out to eat is a true dining challenge. Years ago, it wasn't all that common to see someone leave a restaurant with a "doggy bag." No one was kidding anyone. Fido never saw the contents of that bag.

The bag, though, has been upgraded, and now, as we make a twilight arrival at a favorite eatery, we see a blizzard of white Styrofoam containers floating across the parking lot in the hands of sated customers.

What is going on here? Why are restaurants flying in the face of every diet in the land—and what happened to Aristotle's "moderation in all things?" Why are they not more concerned about all of the statistics that show we are becoming a fatter population? The latest numbers I've seen show that two-thirds of us are overweight or obese.

Is there a food industry plot at work? They must know that we children of depression and WWII parents have been taught to clean our plates. "Children are starving in (insert appropriate country here), and you won't finish your turnips! Shame!"

We are even able to talk ourselves into liking things we really don't, just because they are placed in front of us and some universal rule says we can't let them go to waste.

I was in the kitchen slicing up a lime many years ago. Our youngest son was in a high chair and watched me closely, After a bit, he waved his arms excitedly and said something like "ga ga goo glubble." Surely he didn't want a wedge of lime? I told him as much. "No Curty—you don't really want this!" More arm waving, and "goo gobble gub gub." I finally relented. He began sucking on the lime and his face puckered up like a little prune—but he continued to eat it. I wondered what I had done.

Had I instilled in him a love of fruit or was he headed for a bad relationship with gin and tonics? All I could say for sure, was that it was in front of him and he wanted it.

So—programmed as we are, from an early age, not to waste food, how do we seniors cope with gargantuan restaurant meals that we can't possibly finish? A lot of us have already figured out that if we develop the will to put our knives and forks down early, we can turn our dinner into a two-for-one bargain. And the best and brightest among us have even refined this practice with a brilliant stratagem.

A few weeks ago we were having dinner with one of our couple friends. When our lady companion ordered her dinner— a grilled chicken salad—she asked that a leftovers box be brought with it.

I was puzzled, but soon saw the wisdom in this. When it was put in front of her, she divided it between her plate and the box before she ever sank a fork in her meal. Think about this; she now had a completely unsullied, unmessed-up, un-glopped up (with ranch dressing which she had gotten on the side) meal. "Tomorrow's lunch!" she proudly exclaimed.

I was immediately impressed with this innovation, and my wife and I adopted it from that point on.

Not everyone, though, is able to break the old "clean your plate" habit, and they feel obligated to shovel away until everything is polished off. This has consequences. Experts say that for the first time in history, more people on the planet are dying of overeating than of starvation. Health care professionals sigh about this but don't seem to have any solution.

The Mayor of New York City does, however. Last year he took steps to make restaurants provide information on the calories in their offerings, get trans fats out of them and stop the sale of supersized sugary drinks.

This blew up on him later. He went out for lunch one day not long ago. The restaurant refused to serve him a second slice of pizza, and wouldn't give him a refill on his sweetened ice tea.

Chuck Thurston

When Food Came South

In 1978, IBM opened a new plant in Charlotte, North Carolina. There were a few other IBM locations in the south, but to me, they didn't really qualify as Southern. Raleigh was a provincial capital, filled with bureaucrats, admins and politicians. Boca Raton, Florida, was heavily occupied by Yankee expatriates and northern retirees. But Charlotte—surely here would be a mother lode of genuine southern culture and customs.

I was interviewed for a job in Charlotte, and accepted the offer. My wife and I have been here since.

When you relocate to another part of the planet you take your food habits with you. You hope to find enough of your old preferences to make for a comfortable transition, and you look forward to new culinary discoveries.

I soon found some critical gaps in the supply chain.

I traveled a bit in my new job, and on one walk through the Charlotte airport, ran into a colleague coming back from his own trip. He was carrying a gallon tin of olive oil in each hand. "Tony, what's up?"

"What do they cook with down here, Chuck?"

Ah, yes. We had already discovered that olive oil, if a supermarket carried it at all, was in little 4 oz. boutique bottles. Maybe enough to dress a couple of small salads, but nowhere near enough to dip your dinner bread in and get you through the rest of the week.

That's assuming you could find bread worthy of the name.

When we made our first trips to supermarkets, we discovered almost no bread but gummy white. My Danish wife and her classmates used to play a little game with a slice of the "American bread." They'd peel off the crust and roll the inside up into a marble sized ball.

Where were the hearty ryes, crusty baguettes, or thick, chewy sourdoughs? And where, for god's sake, were the bagels?

This was biscuit country, son! They were everywhere and lathered with everything! They made appearances at breakfast, lunch and dinner. A popular fast food chain served them all day with chicken.

The only pasta we found: elbow macaroni and spaghetti. Where were the penne, the rotini, the orzo, and the farfalle?

Northern companies that built plants in the south, often brought a core of trained and experienced workers down with them to get the new enterprise up and running, before a large contingent of locals were ultimately hired. I was one of the first 600 employees in the IBM plant that eventually peaked at about 4800 workers.

The cafeteria offered familiar fare to lessen the trauma to their Yankee transfers. I was getting my coffee one morning and heard this remark behind me—evidently a response to a "what are these?" question:

"They look like a donut, but they hain't sweet!"

Those boys would have swooned if they knew that there are people who like to top a bagel with smoked salmon and cream cheese—for breakfast, yet! And with coffee!

I was initially puzzled and thought that drinking your morning coffee through a straw was a very peculiar local custom. Soon we discovered what was going on, and were amazed at the number of people—and not just kids, by any means—whose regular breakfast beverage was iced tea or some soft drink! What??

Sure, I thought—cocola over ice after some yard work on a hot day—but as your morning eye opener?

In a related incident, we asked some of our new neighbor friends to join us for pizza and beer at a local restaurant. They ordered pizza and iced tea. I frankly think that combination might be against the law in some Italian neighborhoods in the north. What were these people doing?

Some of the new items I could relate to. Grits I was familiar with. My West Virginia mother routinely served them to us at breakfast, but we ate them like a breakfast cereal, with milk and sugar—or maple syrup—another stranger to most of the grocery stores we visited.

My brother watched me salt and pepper my grits and stir my eggs in them on one early visit. "What are you *doing?*" he asked. When in Rome…

9

Liver mush turned out to be a close cousin of the Pennsylvania Dutch scrapple—concocted from the bits and pieces of the pig not useful for anything else.

About desserts: we soon found out a basic southern mantra regarding dessert: "There isn't hardly anything that can't be improved by adding a few marshmallows!" A sweet potato casserole wasn't even spared. The marshmallow was enshrined in chocolate and sold as something called a Moon Pie. The southern sweet tooth was a wonder to contemplate.

My wife and daughter took a cake decorating class. When I found out that icing was little more than lard and 4X sugar—with maybe a little coloring—I was stunned.

The natives seemed to have an incredible genius for converting an absolutely healthy food into something that would make your cardiologist cringe. Green beans were not worth their time until they had been boiled for three hours with a piece of ham fat. Fish? Deep fry that rascal and serve him up with some hush puppies! Arterial sludge.

My wife and I took our share of twitting from our new Carolina friends and neighbors. Once at a meeting of an outdoor club, one of the club's jokesters asked us, "You know what we say down here when we see a car with Yankee plates pulling a U-Haul?"

"Help is on the way," my wife responded. And it was.

One of the first imports was ol' debbil rum. Yes—towns and counties slowly changed from wet to dry. You no longer had to carry your bottle of booze or wine in a brown paper bag into what billed itself as an otherwise classy restaurant.

On one of our first dining excursions after the new laws permitted liquor by the drink, we ordered wine with our dinner. The waiter dutifully advised us that if we were planning on having two drinks, a bottle might be the more economical purchase. When we agreed, he brought us a two-liter jug. There were certainly locals who could put away this amount of sweet tea at a sitting, and the servers apparently transferred this paradigm to their new beverages.

When we told him we couldn't possibly finish this off, they cheerily brought us two large Styrofoam cups to haul the excess home. This was the routine procedure for iced tea you wanted to take with you—so why not?

But slowly, slowly, other foods began to infiltrate the environment. The bread and pasta aisles in the supermarkets lengthened. Olive oil appeared in big bottles. We found broiled fish options in restaurants.

A street vendor in downtown Charlotte got a vendor's license and sold bagels off a cart in center city. He met his future wife that way, incidentally, and they started a bagel shop together. Oh happy day!

Fast food restaurants began to advertise the superiority of their coffee blends.

Starbucks came to town.

Like Kurtz, who went native in Conrad's *Heart of Darkness*, we made our peace with North Carolina cuisine and assimilated some things we had no prior experience with. We like stewed okra, pinto beans and country steak. We can get passionate over the local barbecue.

But no migration is ever one way. Sooner or later the natives themselves get restless and begin to check out the unknown areas of the map where there be dragons and Yankees with strange food predilections. They are on the move...bagels came down. Biscuits are heading up.

Bojangle's and Krispy Kreme have moved north.

Penne Sans Vodka

At the supermarket one day, my wife picked up a box of our favorite crackers. "Oh look," she said, "They have taken the trans fat out of these!"

This was good news. We have been checking product nutrition labels for some time, and manufacturers seem to be responding to people who are becoming more concerned about the fat, sodium and cholesterol being put in our systems. Every now and then we find that an old favorite has suddenly become healthier! And in almost every case, we haven't missed the things they took out!

We recently discussed this trend with friends over a pizza we had just ordered. We jokingly discussed what could be left off that would make it healthier and still leave it as an identifiable pizza? Cheese and tomatoes seemed to be "givens", but we got various votes to sacrifice pepperoni, salami and ground beef. How low could we go?

It got me thinking. How many of the things we eat would be better for us if it weren't for the "ala's", "and's" and "with's" that we add to them? I composed a simple test.

Look at the list below and pick the part of the food item that is good for you, and the part that will make your doctor frown.

broccoli and cheese sauce
mashed potatoes and gravy
fish and chips
strawberry shortcake
shrimp alfredo
chicken fricassee
crab croquettes.

The answers:
Good for you—broccoli, potatoes, fish, strawberries, shrimp, chicken, crab.
Doctor will frown—cheese sauce, gravy, chips, shortcake, alfredo, fricassee, croquettes.

I saw a pattern here. In every case, the good part was named first. Limit yourself to this part of the recipe, and you would be ok. On the other hand, you might benefit from an accidental omission. Consider this:

One evening we were having dinner at the home of friends. As we were relaxing afterward with coffee, we heard our hostess utter a piteous "Oh no!" from the kitchen. Before we could rouse from our chairs and rush to her aid, she came into the dining room holding a measuring cup of clear liquid and told us that her meal had been a bit fraudulent. "We were supposed to be having 'Penne ala Vodka'" she said. "I am afraid I forgot to put it in. What you just ate was 'Penne sans Vodka!'"

Well, it was an easy mistake to make. She had carefully measured out the booze and set it aside, to add at the appropriate time, but overlooked it at the critical moment. For myself, I was completely happy with what I had been served and told her so. The rest nodded agreement.

I thought about this experience a lot. Shortly afterwards, my wife was contemplating our evening menu and said, "How would you like some macaroni and...."

"Whoa there!" I stopped her in mid-sentence. "Just the macaroni, if you please...forget about the...um...other stuff."

"Hmm...that would be pretty bland, but if you insist, I can just cook up some macaroni for you. I was also thinking of spinach and salmon patties."

"Just plain spinach, I hope—not creamed or anything," I said.

"Just spinach! You know, the leafy green stuff! Think you can handle a little vinegar on it?"

I sensed that she was becoming a bit testy, if not downright sarcastic. But someone had to make the case for good health in this discussion. I did a quick mental assessment of salmon patties. They were really salmon...croquettes! A word on my no-no list! I gently told her so, and she walked away in a huff.

She was right. My dinner was bland. She had her macaroni and...um...stuff, with a delicious looking croquette—I took my little elbows plain with canned salmon. The spinach was lovely—and I felt that I was a better man for my self-control. I congratulated myself on discovering the good food/bad food code.

And then one day I was leafing through a woman's magazine in some doctor's waiting room. Motor Trend had apparently been lifted by another patient. As I casually scanned through some items in a recipe section, I was chilled to read the title of a good looking dish: Beef Burgundy!

When I returned home, I began to rummage through some cookbooks on the shelf. My system crashed and burned before my eyes. Ham hocks and lima beans! Corned beef and cabbage!

Back to the ol' drawing board.

Offing the Boy Friend

Last night my wife said to me, "I have to kill off a boyfriend."

"Well, Paul Simon said there must be fifty ways to leave your lover. I'd stop short of doing him in, though. That seems kind of drastic to me. If you're caught, it sticks me with *all* of the cooking!"

"Oh don't be silly," she said. "This is a character in the new book I'm writing."

"Why do you have to kill him?" I said. "Can't his girlfriend just dump him?"

"It's more complicated than that. They are engaged to be married. But there is a plot twist that makes it unlikely, and well—it would just work better if he was out of the picture—permanently."

"Damn," I said. "You are starting to sound like The Godfather here. I didn't realize that your romantic fiction was so cold blooded."

She ignored me. "The heroine can't move on with her life until he is gone, and it has to be an accident."

"How about a heart attack?" I said. "It happens all the time to guys of his age."

"Her first husband died of a heart attack," my wife said. "I can't very well use that again."

"I see your point, but there are lots of other options," I said. "Automobile, drowning, getting shot, let me count the ways!"

"Well—he lives in Denmark," she said.

"Piece of cake," I said. "You guys never cook anything. You and Gitte used to eat beef tartare all the time. Raw beef with a raw egg yolk! That is just asking for food poisoning!"

She dismissed my argument. "Danish beef is grass fed, so they don't have to load them up with antibiotics. Gitte and I have never had a problem—and look at you! How many times have I seen you put away pickled herring?"

"True, but I washed it down with aquavit. It's a known fact that salmonella can't swim in schnapps."

"Exactly!" she said. "Do you have any more bright ideas?"

"You are going to make this really difficult. We could waste him in a New York minute over here in the states—sure you can't have him on a business trip over here? Why—a little tainted BBQ at some county fair in the U.S., and his girlfriend's worries are over! She can go after that ferry boat captain she wanted in the first place!"

"I thought of sending him on a trip," she said, "but it doesn't work with the rest of the plot."

I gave myself a healthy pour of a good North Carolina merlot and began some serious thinking. Finally, I said, "Ok, let's work on this. Denmark is pretty much surrounded by water. How about you drown him?"

"That's the catch," she said. "Since you are never more than twenty minutes from the ocean anywhere in Denmark, everyone knows how to swim."

"Well, perhaps a shark..."

"I don't think there are any sharks in the Baltic."

"How about he gets caught in a police crossfire, while they are chasing a bank robber?"

"This story takes place in the 1960s," she said. Danish policemen didn't even carry guns then."

"Dearie, you would be better off moving this plot line to the U.S. We could get him shot almost any old place—a movie theater, a Walmart parking lot, a college campus...you name it, we can shoot it up! Are you sure you can't bring him over here to visit an ailing relative—maybe take the afternoon off to catch a movie?"

She ruled all of these scenarios out, and I was getting a little irritated. "Well, I know the Danes have cars—can't we have him get killed in an accident?"

"I thought about that, too, but Denmark has very few traffic deaths. Most people use bicycles for short trips—or the public transportation—busses, trains."

"Oh yeah—I remember trains," I said. "Ran on tracks. Nice big roomy seats. You could get a meal in the dining car and then go back to that seat and take a snooze. Say—how about he is walking across the street and gets hit by a drunken driver!"

16

"Hmmm…drunken driving is pretty rare in Denmark. They don't just pull licenses—they take away your car!"

"Well, I guess that would tend to make you want to bar hop by bus," I said.

I pointed out that U.S. Highways were second to none in road rage—with the weaponry to compliment—and made a few more suggestions, but she did not go for any of them, and insisted that this boyfriend had to meet his Waterloo in Copenhagen. She looked dejected, and I was getting desperate. I didn't want to abandon an automobile as an accomplice in this.

"Say—you mentioned that they do a lot bicycle riding in Denmark. Why don't we have him get hit by a car while he is out biking!"

She thought that this had promise, but pointed out that bicycles have the right of way over almost every other conveyance. "Automobiles, pedestrians—everything defers to the bicycle; and everyone in the country knows this. There are separate sections of the roads for bikes. A bicyclist is very rarely killed by a car."

"But wait," I said. "Suppose it was a foreigner—a tourist! He could be from a country where the auto is king and everything else must revolve around it! Drive-in banks, restaurants, funeral parlors—a country where bicycles and bicyclists are ignored or treated with disdain—where they are viewed as pests on the public highways, routinely ridiculed for their spandex outfits, and run off the road if they dare to slow traffic down!"

"Why…a tourist…that might work," my wife said.

"Great. I knew I could slip an American into this plot!"

Wine Me Up, Wine Me Down

Raise your hand if you remember sitting cross-legged on the floor of somebody's pad—in your hippy threads—smokin', jokin' and passing around a bottle of cheap wine in a wicker basket.

You don't? You didn't? You missed a seminal part of your misspent youth. My condolences.

A good friend of mine went through the jug wine phase in college, but he was smart enough to remain objective through it. He thought that wine had potential, but asked himself—"is this the best there is?" He determined to find out. He made it a mission to become an expert in them. He soon discovered, though, that the world of wines was so vast that he had to specialize. If you want the skinny on the best cabernet sauvignons, ask my pal Jim.

As young marrieds, my wife and I would get one of the Chianti-in-a-basket bottles to accompany a spaghetti dinner with friends. We thought it lent class to the meal and you had a nice artsy candleholder when the wine was gone.

For the most part, though, wine culture wasn't anything either of us was acquainted with. It had high and low associations—it was either the preferred sip of the rich and elegant, or the paper bagged quaff of derelicts living under viaducts.

We had a few casual associations with it. My mother—a stalwart church-goer—was not a tippler by any means, but she had a bottle of Mogen David in a kitchen cabinet. She would occasionally, in the evening, pour herself a small juice glass to sip. It was a dark, sweet potion that I suppose she believed had some medicinal value; bless her heart.

We moved to North Carolina just as the state began returning—yes, returning—to grape growing and wine making on a large scale. The native scuppernong was America's first cultivated wine grape and the Old North State was an important wine making region before prohibition killed the industry in the 1920's.

At that time, grape growing on a commercial scale

disappeared, and tobacco farming grew to become one of the state's most important agricultural enterprises. And then, tobacco took a hit as its associated dangers became publicized. Smoking rates in the U.S. dropped 50% from 1965 to 2005. Once again, an important agricultural mainstay was marginalized by a cultural shift. My wife and I built a little cabin in the foothills of Wilkes County. It turned out to be ground zero for the rebirth of North Carolina's grape growing and wine making industry.

It turns out that the land used for growing tobacco is also ideal for grapes, so it was out with the bright leaf and in with the vines. Also pushing this switch was another cultural change as health-conscious Americans turned to wine as a preferable alternative to the hard liquor and mixed drinks that once dominated happy hour in years past.

Once Junior Johnson tooled these back roads in a souped up Ford, picking up moonshine to be delivered to customers down state. Folks were now pulling into wineries and, after tastings, driving off with their favorites. Out with White Lightnin', in with Pinot Grigio.

And speaking of resilient—a few weeks ago we stopped by a small family owned golf course near Elkin, North Carolina. We had passed by the sign many times and finally decided to check it out in the event we were in the vicinity on a nice day, perhaps with our clubs in the car.

It was an out-of-the-way spot and we were surprised at the nice little facility. The wife told us a little bit about it. "We have been here for a number of years," Wanda said. "We used to raise tobacco on this very land, then that market started to fail. One night my husband and I sat at the kitchen table and talked about our future. I asked him what he thought we should do."

"Build a golf course," he replied.

"I said, 'Sure…' the next morning there were bulldozers moving dirt around, and here we are!"

And, of course, now they are in the perfect industry. They are smack dab in the middle of the Yadkin Valley grape growing region and a lot of the guys and gals who used to drink potent brews out of mason jars are now cultivating a taste for a good merlot or sangiovese. I would guess that a number of them would want to take up pasture pool to complete the makeover.

As all this goes on, we even find ourselves adopting the lingo of the sommelier (that's wine expert to you). Our little steel-roofed cabin has a rain catchment system and every now and then someone will ask us how the water tastes.

We assume a knowledgeable pose, swirl the water glass before sipping, and announce, "Um, yes—well, it has overtones of oak leaves and squirrel dander, with a nice galvanized finish."

This always impresses them.

America's Favorite Drug

A lot depends on how you were first exposed to it. I have a granddaughter whose first experience, for instance, was a very bad trip.

For myself, when I was a little child, the pushers were adults that would try to get me hooked by giving me a spoonful every now and then. They would doctor it up with cream and sugar to make it more appealing to me, and they would be sure to blow on it so it was not too hot. I rather liked the taste, but was probably more taken by the fact that it was a grownup habit that I was being allowed to sample. My wife says this was a part of her own childhood experience in Denmark, so the practice is apparently common in other countries.

But back to my granddaughter's experience:

She came home from school, couldn't find a clean glass right off, so poured her Pepsi in a mug and set it on the kitchen counter. Came back later with her homework and picked up what she thought was her drink.

She got a different fix. It was her mother's left over coffee from that morning. "Cold and disgusting," was the way she described it. She made an on-the-spot decision never to try it again in her lifetime.

Fast-forward a few years. Same girl, same beverage:

I'm so sorry for calling you so many terrible names when I was younger. I do NOT think you are disgusting, rotten, terrible, smelly, or any other foul name. You are sweet nectar sent to us.

Do you see how easily this addiction is possible? After my own first exposure, I didn't bother with it for some time. I drank milk in my boyhood and soda in my teen years—but then came military service and I was hooked just as my granddaughter would be many years later.

What euphoria—what sense of accomplishment and well-being could justify this terrible drive to imbibe it? Once back in civvies, this powerful draw was made clear to me one morning in the cafeteria of the plant I was working in. I was behind one fellow as he drew a king-sized cup of coffee. It was

21

early on a Monday morning. I don't know how his weekend had gone, but as he took a sip, he said, "Ahhh…America's favorite drug!"

I had never looked at it that way, but it made sense to me, and I welcomed the news. I was happier to see an addiction like this embedded in our culture, than that of more noxious substances.

What had happened to my granddaughter and me? How had coffee taken hold in our lives? I'll tell you what happened. In her case it was college courses, late night cramming, finals, etc. I could relate to this. In the military, coffee was almost a rite of passage. It became the potion that got you through the mid watch—from midnight until four a.m.

What a brew it was, though. The last official duty the mess cook performed, before he hit the sack himself, was to fill up the big coffee urn in the hanger and start it brewing—and that's what it did all night.

By midnight it was really ripe, and by three or four in the morning it could pass for asphalt. Let me tell you—if you had to hop on a plane to answer a Search and Rescue alarm at 2 a.m., you were wide eyed, by golly. To make sure that vigilance was preserved, a thermos or two of the stuff went on the plane with you.

I had long since forgotten the spoonful offered me by grownups, and didn't realize that this military concoction bore only a passing resemblance to coffee.

There was a saying at the time that sailors "liked their women like their coffee—sweet and blonde!" Sure. In order to get this stuff down, lots of cream and sugar had to be added. Given that treatment, it could be tolerated.

I drank so much of this hanger coffee, it became my idea of what real coffee actually was. I can't say that I ever enjoyed it—it was a means to the end of staying awake through your watch. I wondered why anyone would drink it voluntarily.

My illusion was so complete that when occasionally, off base, I would get a cup of the civilian version, I would wonder what was wrong with it. Why was it so weak and bland? So lacking in that acidic, bitter quality? Why did it not raise your bile? Could anything this innocuous actually get you through the night? Serious questions these.

In time I realized that what I had been drinking was a horribly defiled version of the real thing. The scales fell from my eyes.

It was not unlike my wife's experience in moving from Pennsylvania to North Carolina. She had come to PA from Denmark via New York, and thought that the world was pretty much defined by cold, damp, dreary weather. I had been south. I told her that there were parts of the country where the sun was known to shine for days at a time. "Get outta here!" she might have remarked, had she been familiar with American idiom at the time.

And so it was with my exposure to real coffee. Had this stuff been around all the time I was swilling the other?

Within just a few years of this cafeteria exchange, I discovered exciting variations on coffee. There were cappuccinos, lattes, mochas—kids seemed to be opting for coffee shop hangouts over soda shops. I could envision my granddaughter hanging out with buds over whipped cream topped peppermint mocha, and it warmed my heart to think of it.

Young couples moving to new locations always check on the amenities near their new digs. Are the schools good? What about police and fire coverage? How about the neighborhood?

Is there a Starbucks nearby?

Chuck Thurston

The Sugar Pie

I grew up without a grandfather in my life. My dad's father died of pneumonia on Christmas Day in 1917. My mother lost her father in 1927. He was in his 40's and another early casualty of the drudgery and toil of the West Virginia coalfields.

I read a lot as a boy, and a wise and kindly grandfather was often a prominent character in these readings. Many of my own boyhood friends told of pleasurable outings with their own grandfathers. I was, frankly, a little sad that I would never be able to look back upon such experiences.

I did, though, have a grandmother—and if fate is going to consign to you a single one such, mine could have been the prototype.

I was the first born of her youngest son. Her oldest son was a confirmed bachelor—lived with, and cared for her—so it was unlikely she would ever get an offspring from that branch of the tree.

It would be fair to say that I was spoiled rotten. In those early pictures, I admit to being a cute little rascal, but heck, most four year olds are rather cherubic anyway. We lived a few blocks from grandma's house in our small Pennsylvania town where I spent my early years—before a move to a farm some miles away.

I spent a lot of time at her house. It was a neat little bungalow on a quiet street. In back she had a small garden, a cherry tree and a chicken coop where she kept a number of bantam chickens.

I was often sent out to collect the eggs—no larger than golf balls. As I think about it now, I am sure she had to adjust her recipes to account for the smaller eggs in the items she baked.

She was a squarish woman—not terribly tall, certainly not fat—and "stocky" doesn't seem to fit her. Sturdy seems appropriate. She had raised four children, alone, in the depths of the depression.

I remember her attending Halloween parties in costume— not that she ever fooled anyone for very long. She laughed a lot—a contagious cackle that soon had those around her laughing along with her, at whatever she had found humorous.

I have many old photos of her. In several she is wearing a plain housedress with an apron. In other pictures, she is obviously dressed for church or some special occasion, wearing a black suit with a small hat on her head. Plain, black no-nonsense shoes in every case.

Grandmothers of her type seem to be extinct now. The media is filled with glamor pusses pointing out that—although their children have indeed had children of their own—they are as hot as ever they were, and are wearing the duds to prove it. My grandma looked like…well…a grandma.

Some of my earliest memories are of sitting in a chair at a table in her kitchen while she baked—and she had an oven that seemed in perpetual use. I would have been around four years old.

She would walk over and bend down—her face close to mine—and say "I am going to make a little sugar pie—just for you!" Then she would turn back to her workstation by the stove and assemble her gift.

The "just for you" was magic. I wasn't the only little prince in our household for very long. I was barely out of diapers before my mother had another heir—and then another—and sharing was the order of the day.

The sugar pie was baked in a small pie tin—perhaps six inches in diameter. It was a thin, sweet, yellowish concoction, almost like very thin custard. I have no idea what it was made of, or how it was made. I have looked at many recipes and pictures of possibilities over the years since, but none seem to hit it on the head. No matter. It was good, and it was mine.

She would place it in front of me. I vividly recall the brown mottling—age spots—on her hands.

She often sang to me:
So, kiss me my sweet,
And so, let us part,
And when I grow too old to dream,
That kiss will live in my heart.

In my toddler's days this was just singing—just a song. As pleasant to my ears as any song directed to a child by a loving adult would be. Many years later I looked up the song. It was popular the year before I was born. I can imagine Emma—bustling about her kitchen—humming it, while I floated in my mother's womb.

It was just for me, too.

YOU HAVEN'T BEEN LECTURED TO LATELY

Buy My Book, Dammit!

I was talking with my wife the other day. "Sooner or later, we have got to start thinking about a new vehicle to get up the hill to our cabin. The minivan isn't much good on those roads and your Subaru is getting old enough to vote."

"Well," she said. "Maybe you can make enough money on your book to buy something."

"That is a harsh scenario," I said. "I know a writer who claimed that after the publisher's cut, the bookstore fee, and the gas he burned to get to book signings, he lost money on every sale. I asked him, 'how do you stay in business?' Can you imagine what he said?"

"I couldn't guess," my wife replied.

"'Volume,' he told me. That was certainly eye opening, but as I thought about it, that remark gave me a great idea. Would you like to hear it?"

"Do I have a choice?"

"My hope is that the more of these books I have out, the better my chances of having something wonderful happen. Because it is so inexpensive, people will be inclined not to keep a really close eye on it.

"Say a guy lays a copy down on the seat next to him in the airport gate area. His flight number suddenly gets announced. He jumps up, grabs his carryon and heads for the gate. My small, lonely volume of the Scribbles is left behind."

"Oh boy," my wife said.

"Hear me out, Dearie. Passengers begin to filter into that gate area for a subsequent flight. A young secretary takes his old seat.

"Now get this. She has just missed buying the last copy of Cosmopolitan at the newsstand after getting all worked up by a front cover blurb on *'100 Different Positions!'* Another woman had grabbed the Cosmo, and headed to the newsstand checkout, taking it right from under her outstretched fingers."

My wife rolled her eyes.

"The secretary is desperate for an inflight read and sees my book on the seat next to her. She looks around, makes a couple of inquiries and determines it's abandoned. Finder's Keepers!

"In route to Los Angeles, she discovers that these Scribbles don't measure up to Cosmopolitan, and shoves the little book in the seat pocket in front of her. There it joins candy wrappers, used napkins and a couple of mini-bottles left from the day's flights."

"Well, when you're hot, you're hot. What then?"

I was on a roll. "Then," I said, "an airline cleanup crewmember finds the book. Hmmm, he muses. Something about seniors. His old Romanian grandfather's birthday is coming up and this looks to be in decent shape. He takes it home, giftwraps it and takes it to the old man's house the next day.

"A few days after this, Woody Allen is in a Hollywood agent's office. He wants a 'distinguished older gentleman' type to play a part in a film he's making. It's about a May-December romance, and he has already signed Scarlett Johanssen—obviously the 'May.' Now he is scouting around for the dead-of-winter role.

"An elderly janitor is emptying wastebaskets in the agent's office. As he bends over to pick up some trash, a slim volume drops out of the back pocket of his coveralls and lands on the floor at Allen's feet!"

"Let me guess," my wife said. "It's your book and the janitor is the old Romanian Grandfather!"

"Yes! It is the old grandfather, all right! But, get this - Woody spots the book and his eyes home in on the graveyard scene. A wilted flower lies atop a fresh grave. A particular cog ratchets up a notch in his brain.

"Woody had figured that he would have Scarlett—at the end—bid a tear-laden graveside farewell to her old lover. But this cover suggests a really bizarre twist! Suppose the May role in this movie actually checks out before the December, so at some point the old gentleman visits his young sweetheart's grave!

"Right there, big as life, are some wilted flowers. He didn't put them there. Who did? Was Scarlett fooling around on him? Was he being cuckolded? His weakened heart skips a beat or two—will he have enough time left to change his will so he can cut her relatives out of it?"

"Well, that would be Woody Allen, alright," my wife agreed. "Are you telling me that he is rewriting his movie while he looks down at the book?"

"Woody has a quick mind. He looks down, picks up the book and finds out that the old janitor is more than happy to take a $50 dollar bill for it.

"Allen runs through my book on the taxi back to his studio office. Nothing there lights his fire, but later, he checks out my Facebook page. Now I might not be the most distinguished older gentleman he has ever seen..."

"No understatement there," from my beloved.

"I'll ignore that," I told my wife, "but I look passable and sufficiently decrepit, so that my anticipated final demise will have some screen cred.

"And consider this—Woody and I are about the same age, and this is the kind of role that he would have taken for himself not so long ago. It's a risky business, though. If your film flops, it suggests to the critics that you can't even direct yourself. If an egg is to be laid, better to get an unknown to do it. He figures, what harm would it do to give this Thurston fellow a screen test?"

"I hate to think where this is going," said my wife.

"Sneer if you want. A week later I am on a plane to Hollywood. My cardiologist has already warned me that shooting love scenes with Scarlett Johanssen may void my health insurance, but I am philosophical about it. Who wants to live forever?

"Now, I am not completely unrealistic. I doubt that Scarlett and I are ever going to be a Hollywood item, but, <cough> one never knows."

"Doubt?" my wife said.

"Well, you don't have to worry. I don't get the role. Scarlett says something to the effect that she wants 'someone willing to die for her—not ready to die on her!' They fly in

29

Sean Connery from Scotland—who looks, incidentally, even more decrepit than I—and has even less hair. He has a lot more panache though, and has apparently ignored any warnings his cardiologist might have given him. To my chagrin, Scarlett is relieved at the substitution. I fly home, overlook this slight and don't let it dampen my ambition."

"So where," said my wife, "does big money come in here?"

"I get an expense account for my trip. I carry my own tea bags and instant oatmeal—and I get back with some jingle left over. Woody also feels obligated to compensate me for use of the cover idea."

"Go thank your son," said my wife. "It was the cover that did the work. None of your scribbles."

"I will overlook that sarcasm, but all told, my take would be enough to get me a good used Subaru Forester and I would be able to climb the mountain—safely—to my cabin."

"I hate to delude you any further," said my wife. "You're doing a pretty good job on your own, but I wouldn't pin my hopes on some pipe dream like this! If that Walmart greeter job is still open, you might want to check there!"

I ignored this insult, rose from my chair and walked to the windows overlooking the Brushy Mountains. I raised my head high and clasped my hands behind my back, as I gazed at this vista. I sighed deeply. I imagined this would be the pose that successful writers might take if considering plots. If I'd had a pipe I would have clenched it between my teeth to complete the effect, but I stopped smoking some years ago.

My mind wandered briefly off topic to consider whether an electronic pipe might be marketable, but a grand finale to my story was beginning to form.

"Suppose," I said, "Woody's project is less than successful. But imagine—working on the set is an associate producer who was heavily invested in the film. He is disappointed at his poor return, and thinks that if this film were in the hands of a better director, he could be bankrolling a blockbuster. And—check this—he just happens to play golf once a week with—you're going to love this—Stephen Spielberg! Now—can you guess what happens next?"

I turned around—triumphantly—to confront her, but she had left the room.

Look, I hate it that writers are reduced to such shameless self-promotion. Believe me, I'm just as embarrassed about it as you are—but The Kardashian Girls have set the bar so low, that it is no effort at all to hop over it.

Buy my book, dammit!

Chuck Thurston

You've Come A Long Way Kid

When I was a young boy, there were two statements I could make to my parents that meant absolutely nothing to them:

"I don't like that."

"I don't want to do that."

The first statement was simply ignored. The bowl of turnips would be passed around the big farmhouse table, I would get a healthy dollop on my plate alongside my mashed potatoes and chicken, and that would be that. If I, or my brothers, didn't clean things up we would be reminded that the "children in China would be happy to have food like this."

I would have been more than willing to donate my turnips, but that was never an option given me.

I am pretty sure I never made the second statement more than once or twice. I quickly learned that "I don't want to do that" was met with stunned silence and a look of disbelief— actually, more like non-comprehension. What did not wanting to do something have to do with anything?

My father's father died when my dad was 14, and he became one of the primary providers for his family at that age. Mom's mother died birthing a 10th child when Mom was five, her coal-miner father when she was 14. She spent her early years shuttling between relatives, and was on her own by 17.

Our farm day started and ended with feeding the chickens, milking the cows and slopping the hogs. When the animals were taken care of, the other businesses of the season were attacked: plowing, planting, cultivating, mowing, haying, equipment repair and other such tasks.

To be sure, this routine was often relieved by games. In the summer, one of my dad's favorites was "skip the bean," and the rules were simple. We merely went to the rows of Kentucky Wonder Blue Poles in the vegetable garden and pulled every green thing in sight—with careful orders to "skip the bean." In the evening, Mom was not about to cater to individual eating peccadilloes in a family of seven. Her game was "stretch the bean." Baked beans not eaten at the evening meal were going to be in our school sandwiches under a thick slice of onion the next day.

Things were rarely put to me as suggestions or recommendations. This held true later in my military sojourn. "You men *will...*" was often the preface to some order or another.

A fellow I used to carpool to work with told me the story of how he broke a bad cigarette addiction. His doctor told him, after a checkup, "You should really stop smoking, Clem."

Clem replied, "I can't work with your recommendation. You're my doctor. If you think I should stop smoking, order me to do it."

The doctor, taken aback, consented. "Ok, as your personal physician, Clem, I am ordering you to stop smoking for your health's sake." He added, "...and since you are really hooked, I am giving you a prescription for a tranquilizer to help you through it."

"Give me two prescriptions," Clem said. "My wife is going to quit too!"

I more or less grew up with these models until a burger purveyor some years back notified me that I "deserved a break today." That got me thinking, and I began paying attention to other commercial messages that I was getting, and found what seemed to be a common theme.

The folks trying to sell me stuff were making the case that I would not merely be better off for buying their products, but that no one had the right to deprive me of their offerings!

One law firm was telling me that I should be getting the money "I deserved" for whatever ailed me. Yet another bunch of lawyers advised me to, "Make sure you get what's owed to you!"

An auto manufacturer told me I might be one of the lucky people who had "earned the right" to drive their new luxury car. "Everyone deserves a good meal," a restaurant let me know. Amazing.

A cell phone company: "You deserve unlimited data, unlimited time, unlimited coverage!"

Gosh, I wish I had known about this theory of deservedness when I was a boy. I might have been able to establish that I was owed a whole lot better deal on farm chores; and let my

mother know that I really deserved better than turnips.
Maybe not.

Advice For The Young'uns

This is for you young folks—not yet done with your schooling. You others can go do something else. Get a six pack out of the fridge and go to the garage. See if you can find that rattle in the family jalopy that your wife has complained about—for six months. This is a column on good advice that you were offered years ago, and rejected. How do I know this? If you had taken it, you'd be highly results oriented, driving a new car and you'd have cut back on drinking.

So gather around kids.

Sooner or later you will get some graduation advice. Perhaps you have already had some. It seems to start earlier now. I've even heard of kindergarten graduation ceremonies. The earliest events are mostly just exercises in telling you what a good little student you have been—how much your teachers have enjoyed having you around. You get a pat on the head before you skip out into the freedom of summer.

But things become more serious as you get older.

High school graduation ceremonies become more about the future that is in store for you. You notice that the path is seldom seen as smooth. Times are always difficult. Courage and dedication will be necessary. Your commencement speaker is generally an educator, businessman, religious figure, artist or entertainer. It doesn't matter. You will never hear that the economy is booming, jobs are for the taking, peace will guide the planet and love will steer the stars.

Nonetheless, with courage, dedication, etc., etc., you will soldier on. The pat on the head has become a pat on the back. Sometimes it feels suspiciously like a shove. You can almost imagine school maintenance coming in the back door as you are herded out the front, re-oiling the floors and dusting off the desks for the next set of prisoners as they release you and your cohorts.

College commencement addresses introduce a dire new note. The speaker will say, sometimes with surprising candor, that you must fix the world that his or her generation is handing off to you. In other words, these people who have been presented to you as role models—people you've been taught to admire for their business acumen, spiritual advice, and wisdom—are essentially admitting they are flops in the game of life. They are tossing the ball to you and heading for the locker room.

Now this is a harsh statement, but I am not calling graduation speakers misleading liars. In a sense they are trapped in their rhetoric. I give you Thurston's Law:

1)Humans can rationalize *any* human behavior.

2)It follows, then, that the response to any statement or question regarding human behavior is *"It depends."*

3)Since language is finite, "it depends" advice is invariably presented in *clichés and platitudes.*

Oh sure, psychologists and philosophers have their dictionaries of terms, but your speakers will never resort to these arcane descriptors to explain what you must do. They probably don't understand them themselves.

I once asked a priest why the Catholic Church took so long to move from Latin to the vernacular. "We didn't think you were smart enough to understand it," he said—meaning that since we couldn't comprehend these great theological mysteries anyway, it didn't matter in what language they were presented (Thurston's Law #1). Now old Father Jim was a Jesuit, after all—and he said it with a wink—but still...

Here is the great irony in the advice offered in these speeches: All of it is right! Every blessed piece of it! You are not being led down the garden path (as an old cliché puts it) by any of these folks. It is just that clichés and platitudes are certitudes—and, yet, as I have just informed you (Thurston's Law #2), the advice you get...well, it depends!

I'll give you a simple example: One speaker may counsel, "haste makes waste!" and another, "he who hesitates is lost!"(T's Law #3). Both of these are wonderful pieces of advice! But—which one should you take? Well, it depends! (T's Law #2).

Last year I was talking to an old friend whose son had just graduated from high school.

"That graduation speaker was wonderful," he said. "Lots of

good advice for those kids!"

"That's great," I replied. "Who was it?"

"Some doctor so-and-so. I forget his name. Told them a lot of stuff about taking good care of themselves so they would have a lot of energy to get stuff done."

"Ahhh," I said. "That would be the old 'better health for a better life' pitch. Very appropriate for a doctor. What kinds of suggestions did he make?"

"Eat right, get a lot of exercise. He even got me excited about getting back in my program at the Y! He also said a good night's sleep was very important. 'Early to bed and early to rise' he said...and this doctor got so poetic, I started taking notes." My friend pulled a tattered scrap of paper out of his wallet and began reading.

"Listen to this," he said. "'Even a soul submerged in sleep, is hard at work and helps make something of the world.'...'a well-spent day brings happy sleep at night' ...Don't you think those are the kinda things those kids should hear?"

"Well, that depends," I said (Thurston's Law #2). "Doesn't Donnie work 2nd shift now?"

He said that was so.

"Won't work," I said.

Chuck Thurston

Up Close and in Your Face

Back in the 1930s, Joe Louis, having been hammered by Max Schmeling in their first fight, came looking for blood in the rematch. His onslaught was fast and brutal. Spectators at ringside said later that Schmeling bellowed in pain as Louis slammed a vicious blow to his body. The sound is not heard above the crowd's roar on any of the grainy films of the event. You had to have been there to catch it.

A few years ago, highly directional microphones began picking up the action during professional football games. For the first time, people—other than the players—could hear the quarterback's signals, the grunts and labored breaths of charging linemen, the clash of pads and helmets. Many fans that had never seen the action closer than a television screen or from the upper sections of the grandstand were surprised by the audible violence of the game.

Unless we have played some of these games at a reasonably high level of proficiency, it is hard for us to truly appreciate how fast, strenuous, violent—and yes, beautiful—the effort is, and the pain and exertion necessary to excel at it. We enjoy the game as spectators, only "seeing as through a glass, darkly."

Sometimes we can come close to the reality. Many years ago, there was a pitching machine in Brooklyn's Coney Island—probably there's still one there. You could select one of several major league stars of your era to hit against. I dialed in Rip Sewell, a successful relief specialist for the Pittsburgh Pirates. No one had ever hit a home run off his famous "blooper ball"—until Ted Williams parked one in right field in the 1946 All Star game.

I managed to foul off a couple off Rip's offerings and then decided to try and get my bat on one of Don Newcombe's fastballs. The audio version of this would have been something like "Whoosh...Whifff"—*twice*. I never got my bat off my shoulder for the *first* pitch.

Years later, my wife and I took tennis lessons. Our instructor was a young man who had had good success in local tournaments. He served up softballs and patty-caked his returns to give us hackers a shot at hitting something. Before our last session was over, I asked him to serve to me as he would if he were playing in an honest-to-gosh tournament.

I crouched behind the baseline, waving my racket and rocking from side to side as I had seen the pros do. He rose up on tip-toes, brought his racket up from the vicinity of his heels, and tossed the ball up in the air as his racket described a high arc over his head. The sound of this embarrassing moment was something like "Thwack...Whoosh!" My racket flapped helplessly in the breeze generated by his serve.

I am nothing if not persistent, though. Along about that time, I was in a senior basketball league, and not doing too badly until the college kids got out of school for the summer and began to be added to some of the rosters. One evening I was bringing the ball up and looking for an open man when I noticed that the tall and lanky opposing center was playing a very high post. Hmmm, I thought...I bet I can drive the baseline on this kid.

Ha!

As I circled and went up for my modest baseline jumper, I was aware that spider-man had recovered very quickly. Two long-legged steps had put him in position to smash the ball right back in my face. I was really mad. This was a low-key adult recreational league, after all, and I snapped at him angrily. "We are supposed to be playing this game for fun!" I said.

He grinned broadly—"*That* was fun!" I had to concede that he had a point there—from *his* perspective!

But despite many efforts with cameras and microphones to give us a better feel for the action, we are remote observers—appreciative and impressed with the skill and enthusiasm of the participants, but isolated from the nuances of the real experience.

I have taken granddaughters to see *The Nutcracker* around Christmas time on several occasions. The beauty and energy of these performers is spellbinding—and anyone claiming they aren't athletes will get an argument from me.

Some years ago, some couple friends of ours went to see the great Russian ballet dancer, Mikhail Baryshnikov perform. The wife is a former ballerina herself and a teacher of others. They got seats in the second row.

At some point in the performance, Baryshnikov began a dramatic move near stage front. Our friend's husband felt moisture on his face and wondered briefly what was going on. Then he realized...as Baryshnikov whirled, a halo of droplets orbited out from his spinning form.

Sweat! The Great Baryshnikov was sweating! Imagine that!

Potholes On Memory Lane

Every now and then I get one of those "Remember When" emails—usually from an old classmate.

Typical: "Nobody in your neighborhood locked their doors," "Everybody's mom was home when they got home from school," "You and your girlfriend went 'steady' and getting 'cooties' was your greatest fear." The script is usually accompanied by a 1950's sound track—Dean Martin, Teresa Brewer, Perry Como doing the popular tunes of that period.

The intent is to remind us of how good we had it, in what were supposed to be simpler times. They extol the honesty and virtue of "back then" and complain about how far we have fallen since.

I am old enough to have lived through that particular era, and I know about the experiences of older friends and relatives from earlier years. I don't buy most of this nostalgia. There are a lot of potholes and speed bumps on memory lane.

"If it was good enough for Paw-Paw, it's good enough for me!" I once heard someone say. Maybe so, but my grandfather had to put up with a lot of stuff I blessedly don't. He worked like a mule in the West Virginia coalmines. He lived in a company shack and was paid in scrip—negotiable only at the company store. His wife died in 1918 during childbirth—complicated, no doubt by the flu epidemic of that year. No flu shots then.

My grandfather died in his 40's of some unspecified disease—his illness more than likely complicated by black lung disease. No OSHA, either, or EPA to watch out for poor workers like him.

This was pre-Social Security and Medicare, too. Had he survived, he would have faced his old age coughing up what was left of his lungs in dog-bone poverty.

"Going out to dinner was a real family treat," another piece of nostalgia tells me, but it depended. The wrong skin tone kept you out of a lot of restaurants. It also kept you in second-rate schools with second hand books. Many country clubs and fraternal organizations were picky about a prospective candidate's religion and ethnic origin.

A lot of women's' jobs dried up after WWII, when returning servicemen had to be put to work, and one paycheck would do the job.

But Mom was often home because of limited job opportunities—none paying her as much as a man doing similar work. Women who dreamed of professional careers often found their choices limited. A bright young woman teller, who aspired to a bank presidency, wouldn't have had a prayer in the 1950's.

If you were gay, you were so deep in the closet you were lucky to get fresh air.

How many poor souls carried the angst and resentment created by these social slights around with them for years? A lot, no doubt, but in a market driven society, no need goes unmet.

On the spot to fill these potholes in memory lane were the psychoanalysts—the brainchild of Sigmund Freud—and the psychiatrists. They had been around for a while—"shell shocked" World War I vets were early recipients of the treatment, and it was popularized in novels, films and in the press and among artists. After World War II, the practice expanded greatly. Once the trendy treatment for rich neurotics, psychiatry began to look to the booming middle class.

The problem was that Freud figured that almost everything wrong with you could be traced to your sexual hang-ups. Not so coincidentally perhaps, blame for many of those hang-ups could often be laid at the door of one particular person! My own mom used to recite this with a laugh:

"Who tucked you in your little bed?
Your Mother.
Who kissed you on your little head?
Your Mother.
Who wiped your nose when it had snot?
Who sat you on your little pot?
Who *made* you poop, when you could *not*!
Your *Mother!*
Well, this was patently—my apologies, mom—a bunch of

crap. It was part of the larger zeitgeist that neatly bundled up a lot of racism, sexism, ageism—prejudices of every stripe—economic exploitation, political malfeasance and just plain bad manners—and blamed it on the personal shortcomings of easy targets.

Those mommies, by the way, were busy manning the home front, the factories and raising the kids—while brothers, fathers, sons and hubbies went off to battle—often in company with men and women of different races and sexual orientations.

The psychiatric profession expanded its arsenal with its embrace of psychopharmacology, beginning in the 1950s. New weapons to mollify the disenfranchised! Mommy didn't need a job, birth control or equal opportunity—she needed a Valium!

Eventually the coin of psychoanalysis lost its luster. Gays, Feminists, minorities of every variety, and others who recognized cultural mistreatment when they saw it, were part of the pushback.

I recently paid a visit to my old hometown. The high school I went to is being torn down. It sits on a bluff overlooking the winding Susquehanna River—a lovely location. I understand that apartments and condos will be built on the site. Several alumni friends have sent me pictures of the razing, and I took a few of my own while there.

Many classmates mentioned their sadness as they watched this take place. They recall the fun and laughter—the football games, the pep rallies, and the school dances. But if my high school was typical, this recollection isn't unanimous.

There were always—and remain so today—the awkward boys with few social skills, or the shy girls waiting for the prom invitation that never comes. Not so much shunned, as ignored—by their more popular, prettier, more athletic cohorts. High school is not everyone's bowl of cherries.

Some years ago, Carly Simon sang a song with the line, "These are the good old days." I agree. Recollections of those older times and adventures are fun—they are nice places to visit, but I wouldn't want to live there.

Let's go over to Johnny's Tavern and play "Moments to Remember" on the jukebox. I'll buy you a beer.

Borrowing Time from the Boredom Bank

Morris Twigg cornered me in the supermarket the other day and complained, "I am busier now than I have ever been! How did I get everything done before I retired?" I could identify. The days don't seem long enough.

We checked out our groceries and headed for the parking lot. Morris's son was slouched behind the wheel waiting for his dad. The son's name is Ferdi—short for Ferdinand. I make every attempt to be civil to him, but I am not sure if manners and empathy resonate with him.

As we approached the car, I could see ripples in the asphalt radiating from the bass vibrations of the car's stereo, and could hear—but not comprehend—what sounded like bad poetry set to non-music. Always eager, though, to bridge the generational divide, I smiled, and—as Ferdie cranked the amp back a couple of hundred decibels to permit conversation—asked him how he was doing. "Bored, dude...nothing to do." And he looked it.

I was tempted to lecture Ferdie—gently—but held my tongue. My wife is always chiding me for giving unsolicited advice. "You will never get people to change by telling them what to do," she scolds, and names a long list of my failed suggestions: Floss your teeth, stop biting your nails, start exercising, etc.

"I don't care whether they follow my advice or not," I explain. "It makes me feel better to tell them what they ought to be doing!" She sighs and walks away.

Because of her long insistence that my suggestions for improvement are useless, I decided to take another tack with Ferdie. I realized that though his condition is untreatable, it can be accommodated—and might actually be put to good use.

"Ferdie, how often are you bored during the day?"

He seemed surprised at this, but replied, "*All* day, man...this town is loser city!"

I did some quick calculating. Subtracting time for eating, sleeping, umm—Ferdie has about eight hours of time each day that someone else could easily use.

"Ferdie, how would you like to deposit your unused time in

the Boredom Bank? Other folks could borrow this time and put it to good advantage! They could read the books you aren't interested in, take the trips you find dull, do the exercises you can't work up energy for, chase the pursuits of happiness you lack the spunk to try! What do you say?"

His dad was immediately interested. "Could I...um...borrow..? There's a cruise that Herthel and I would *love* to..."

"Of course! That's the beauty of this plan!"

Ferdie looked plainly unconvinced, "What do I get out of this, dude? No way I just give up my time for *nuthin'*. Banks pay *interest,* man!"

"You are right, Ferdie, and I have thought of that. If you deposit that time, you will no longer have to listen to lectures on how to use it constructively!"

Ferdie perked up at this. His perpetual teenage sulk turned into a wary smile. I knew I had struck a chord with him.

"Now just a minute," said his dad; "I think he ought to be told..."

I shushed him up right away. "Trust me on this one."

Recession Winter Blues

I saw my father cry just once in my life. It was Thursday, April 12th, 1945. I was 10 years old, and was shocked at the sight. He came into the kitchen of our farm house carrying his lunch bucket—home from his work as a machinist at a local factory. They were called war plants in those days. He told us, as he wept, that President Franklin Roosevelt had just died.

My father didn't show strong emotion over many things. He was almost a prototype of the strong, silent type. He had seen a lot in his 42 years. His father died when he was 14 and he left school to help care for his mother and siblings. His first wife died of tuberculosis, leaving him a young widower. He met my mother, married, and had five sons. He went through the depression.

He had no problem with Roosevelt's depression projects and other measures—he had worked on a CCC "bean gang" to keep bread on the table when no other work was to be found. He was also ok with the Federal Deposit Insurance Corporation, and Social Security, which his elderly mother— my grandmother—was now able to collect.

The wealthy and privileged—the "captains of industry" did have problems, however. They vilified Roosevelt—labeling him a socialist and class traitor. My father and other working men and women didn't fall for it. They knew that FDR's programs were no more socialistic than the public funding of our military was socialized defense. Tom Brokaw titled his book of that period, *The Greatest Generation*. They may have been one of the smartest, too.

They took "E Pluribus Unum" a lot more seriously than we do today. The depression had taught them that though we might have come here on different ships, we were all in the same boat now. They believed that the Constitutional injunction to *promote the general welfare* meant just that.

When I was a child of 5 or 6, World War II had just started up. It has been given some credit for ending the depression, but leftovers of the slump were still around in the very early 1940s.

We lived in a house not far from the railroad tracks and on

a couple of occasions, men riding the rails—hobos, they were called—came to our back door to ask my mother if she could spare a bite to eat. I remember one of these men sitting at our kitchen table working on a cup of coffee and piece of pie that my mother—who took her Christian duty seriously—provided.

My paradigm of hard times was thus formed by older experiences. I remember the vivid pictures of the great depression of the '30s. I remember the unshaven, despondent men in slouch hats selling apples or standing in line for a soup kitchen. I recall the images of gaunt women in plain patterned dresses, anxiety etched on their faces, holding hungry children in their arms.

My wife and I are lucky. We both retired after long years of successful employment during good economic times. As long as Medicare and Social Security remain solvent, we can live— if not in luxury—in comfort adequate for our needs.

We know, though, that numbers don't lie. The national unemployment rate has been hanging around eight or nine percent for a long time—and there are regions where it is much worse. The 21st century hobos—and I mean no disrespect by the term—are standing on major intersections with hand painted signs announcing their despair. Fakes you say? Sure— some are, but I'm guessing the percentage is no greater than the corporate shills masquerading as politicians.

What brought this on? For one thing, everything is mobile. Jobs, materials, technology and capital can go anywhere on the planet, and they have. Manufacturers are chasing cheap labor around the globe to fill jobs that will never be coming back to America.

The only thing that's pretty tough to move is us. We tend to want to stay here in the U.S., even as the new entrepreneurs subtly remind us that we are a drag on profit margins. Nobody has outright said—yet—that we ought to be ashamed of our cranky insistence on a living wage, decent housing and affordable health care—but the situation reminds me of the sarcastic comment that W.E.B. Du Bois once made to his fellow blacks: "How does it feel to be a problem?"

You can be forgiven if you are starting to suspect that a dynamic similar to that of over 75 years ago might be going on now—or that you and your family's interest might not be the highest priority in the average corporate boardroom. No—it doesn't seem like a recession to many of us. TV isn't showing us long bread lines of desperate men, no shadowy figures huddled around small campfires in the train yards, but something is out there.

Just a couple of years ago, the corporation that owned the factory where my father worked during the war, moved its corporate jurisdiction to Ireland—from Hamilton, Bermuda. No hurricane threats, and better pubs, I suppose—and Ireland had just moved ahead of Bermuda as the preferred haven for avoiding those pesky U.S. corporate taxes. You know—the ones that many business interests have convinced you cost jobs for American workers. The company stayed below the radar on this issue, since they had already shipped most of their manufacturing to China. "Take the money and run," as the saying goes. Those who are exhorting us to "take back America" might want to look into this hemorrhage of the national treasury.

The execs and their families will love Ireland. It has publically funded health care for all residents—and they qualify—for as long as they are there. The execs and their resident families—their children and grandchildren—will have it.

Your congressional representatives have it, too.

But not you and yours. Not unless *you* do something about it, Citizens. Mr. Smith isn't going to Washington anymore.

Facebunk

The job market is tough for young people these days. A lot of the entry-level jobs have gone overseas. The country is just now beginning to climb out of a bad recession. Many of our young folks will be graduating from high school this spring. This column is for them.

Listen up kids. This is Grandpa. Put down that cell phone for a minute or two and read some advice. Yeah, I know. What can you learn from some old geezer who doesn't even know how to tweet? Tweet, schmeet. Let me explain. I spent 40 plus years in the business world. I have hired people, and fired people. Trust me on this one, gang.

Technology has made it easier than ever to find and keep a job suitable to your talents. It has also made it a whole lot easier to blow a good job chance, or lose the one you have.

First things first. The interview is important. Spend a little time beforehand learning something about the company and the job you are interviewing for. They probably have a certain way they want people to dress, behave, and perform on their jobs.

Google them. You can really impress the dude or dudette giving the interview if you know something about what they do and how they do it.

Be clean and neat and on time for the interview. Smile and make eye contact. Sure, you might be a little nervous—that's to be expected. No big deal. I will tell you a little secret. A lot of times the interviewer is a little nervous too!

Turn off your cell phone and stick it in your purse or pocket. I said OFF, kids—not on vibrate. If I'm interviewing you and I notice you glancing down periodically to scope out your buds…you are cooked. My theory is that if you can't stay untexted for the length of a half-hour interview, I am not going to trust you to give your undivided attention to the position I am looking to fill. Do you want a job, or do you want to spend most of your time playing thumb-doodle? If your answer is "IDK…" you should seriously reexamine your life.

After the interview, be patient. They probably won't make a decision right away, but will let you know in a few days.

What do you think they are doing in the meantime? Fixing up a nice office for you? OMG, no, kid. They might have other people they want to talk to about this job—and they are probably doing a little checking on your references. WTF? Yes, kids. They might want to have a chat with any bosses you worked for before: how you did on the job, why you left, etc. I've had many an enlightening chat with the former employers of folks who wanted a job with me.

A new little wrinkle that might concern you: a lot of them are now looking you up on Facebook, just for the fun of it. This can be a real showstopper for you. Let me explain:

Does your Facebook profile list some of your favorite interests as: "Bud Lite, Miller Lite, Coors Lite, ha ha ha!" This is Facebunk. If I were a prospective employer looking at this, I'd be saying, "Not on MY time clock, dawg!"

Don't list all of your bad habits, no matter how sexy, tough, macho, clever or hilarious you think they are. If those really ARE your primary interests, your new boss will find out about them soon enough. Then you can try to explain why a high flyin', loveable goofball cut-up like you deserves to be working for him or her.

Oh yeah, and kids—while you're at it—apply the granny test to the pics on our Facebook page. If you'd be embarrassed to show them to grandma, grandpa, your pastor or other responsible, respectable folks—dump them. I would delete such pics as: high times with stoner friends, clothing optional parties, various hormonal and testosterone driven activities, mistreatment of animals, small children and other hijinks. More Facebunk. Keep these in your scrapbook. Perhaps when your own grandchildren come along many years from now, they will be enlightened enough to chuckle over them. Perhaps. Assuming you survived them.

Never announce your job interview plans, or preferred job choice to the world. Just like the forward pass in football, three things can happen—and two of them are bad.

A: Best case scenario—you get the job you want, your new employer checks your Facebook and is impressed by your high opinion of them.

B and C suck.

B: Ok, you get the job you want and thumb your Facebook nose at the other employers you interviewed with. These others see your FB entry, and start to wonder, "Hey, why is this guy/gal dissing us? On Facebook, no less!" You can guess where this puts you if you go looking for another job in the future. Computers have long memories. Data is forever.

C: Your announced favorite *doesn't* hire you and the others start to wonder, "Hmmm...wonder why they didn't hire that guy/gal...maybe we should take a closer peek at those references..."

But let's say you're now on the job and you resisted the temptation to exercise options B and C above. Here's some advice on how to keep it.

Never, EVER, diss your place of employment or supervisor on Facebook. Jeez, grow up kids. Nobody really cares if you don't get along with the Chief of the Burger Crew—except the Chief. If he or she finds out that you've made nasty comments on Facebook, OMG!—you are *so* busted, kid.

And in that same vein—never diss a job you left! "WHAT!" you say? "But that was a lousy job and they treated me like crap!" Maybe. (...or maybe you did a less than super-duper job...just sayin'). Why should you care if these yamheads see your insults? Listen, kid. Companies change, bosses change—YOU change. Maybe a year from now you will be looking for another job—with THEM! Remember that computer memory? Never burn your bridges behind you!

It's a jungle out there, gang.

Kindling

You get what you don't pay for.

As Einstein noted, everything is relative. That includes writing skill. A culture is sufficient unto itself—another way of saying that if your writing works for you, and those you are writing to or for, then it's doing the job ok.

Now a culture, within itself, recognizes good and bad writing. So we English speaking folks consider Shakespeare a great writer. Ditto Hemingway and Jane Austen and Mark Twain and many others. I won't get into great writers like Tolstoy or Flaubert—they were translated into stuff that *we* like, but their Russian or French cohorts might have considered them hacks, for all I know. Then some obscure translator, working thanklessly, in a garret, for peanuts, turned them into works that the English market went for.

I bought an eBook reader—one of those little devices that displays books and other internet downloads. My eyes aren't what they used to be, and I can blow up the font on this little device to proportions that I hope will let me get a little more mileage out of my peepers.

I soon discovered a whole new world of reading. These devices have apparently made it possible for anyone to publish almost anything. I foolishly thought that Facebook had cornered the market on drivel, but not so. If you, by chance, are currently reading this on one of the eBook readers, feel free to nod your head right now—but smile—please.

If you think that anyone publishing anything is a scary thought—you are absolutely right. A little of this has always been going on, but a serious investment was usually required of the aspiring authors. You had to go to one of the vanity presses, and lay some money up front to get your work in print. After parents, other relatives, and a few close friends had made obligatory purchases—unless you were foolhardy enough to give them complimentary copies—you were left with a pallet load of books stored in the guest room that you had to unload at cut rate prices to recover costs.

You often did not, and your priceless insights, matchless

humor and inspirational treasures were denied the greater audience that they deserved. This may, in fact, be the fate of this very scribble you are reading!

Many things on the eBook readers are very inexpensive because they are print-on-demand. The publisher doesn't pre-print a lot of books that gather dust in a warehouse until, having failed to excite the book buying public, the books finally wind up on the clearance table in your local bookstore.

Inexpensive (not to say cheap) appeals to me, so I went hunting. I like science fiction stories and began to search for them. How can you go wrong by downloading a sci-fi story that costs you only a buck or two? Or try one for nothing! That's right! Nada, zilch—not a penny! That's exactly what I did! But—to paraphrase the Romans, "Let the non-buyer beware!"

I am reluctant to criticize another writer. So I won't. But in a long, puzzling afterward to his work, the author of the book I downloaded admitted that in this—his first effort—he wanted readers to read his book as if they were watching a TV series or a movie. Exactly—so I view this as criticizing a screenwriter. Fair game.

I don't write movie reviews, but if I did, here's what I'd have to say about this, if I saw it screened:

"Star Trek meets Love Boat, in an adolescent, techno-geek gamer wet dream, that features periodic galactic battles, using incomprehensible weaponry—fought between a Kumbaya crew and fascist corporate goons—and interspersed with long episodes of space ship interior decorating."

If the author had played this work for laughs, he might have concocted one of the great satires of our age, but he also admitted in his afterward, that upon its publication, he wept at re-reading some of his passages in print.

Well, I did too. Tears were rolling down my cheeks at some of his descriptions.

Look, it's been a hot, slow summer. You've had enough of Faulkner and Wharton. Even Parker and Connelly and Grisham are getting a little predictable. You need some lightweight reading. If you have an eBook reader, look up some of this gratis stuff.

Think of it this way—you won't have to bug anyone to get your money back—and no trees are sacrificed in their publication.

Take Two of These and Keep Your Mouth Shut

When early explorers in the new world saw the natives chewing the bark of willow trees to relieve headaches, they scoffed. They ridiculed any kind of cure that didn't involve sin, repentance or your astrological sign. So much for Middle Age treatments. It turns out that these savages were practicing homeopathic medicine. Willow leaves contain salicin—a chemical similar to the acetylsalicylic acid in aspirin. Take that, white man.

Homeopathic—or alternative—medicine operates somewhat on the principal that what doesn't kill us, makes us stronger. Euell Gibbons (*Stalking the Wild Asparagus*) was a great believer. He observed lumberjacks eating tiny quantities of new poison ivy leaves in the spring to create an immunity that would protect them when they ran into the vines in the course of their work. He ultimately got the courage to try this himself and claimed that he could wade through thickets of the stuff with impunity.

I have hung out with Danes quite a bit and long observed them routinely tossing back a shot of Gammel Dansk at breakfast. Gammel Dansk—literally, "Old Danish," tastes roughly like what I imagine an asphalt driveway would, if I were to lick it on a hot Carolina afternoon. It is a 39% alcohol bitters, but it is nicely balanced by cheese and rye bread at breakfast. The Danes always push back from the table none the worse for the experience and ready to take on the day.

The Italians have a similar potion named Fernet-Branca. I think I can identify the essence of shoe polish in it. I don't know what the Italians wash down with this stuff, but I understand that it is frequently put in coffee in the morning to counteract the effects of too much *La Dolce Vita* of the night before.

Both of these concoctions are made from various herbs in closely guarded formulas—and you would not willingly drink either of them unless they had medicinal value.

Now, on the other hand, I fondly recall taking a tablespoon or two of paregoric to fix a bad stomach when I was a younger fellow. It had a licorice-like taste, and your gullet felt as if warm little elfin fingers were massaging it, as it coursed toward your tummy. There were rumors of people getting hooked on it, but I can think of worse addictions. It was extracted from flowers, too. Ok, so they were opium poppies.

A few years ago, I saw a doctor when I was once more having stomach problems. I told him that in my younger days, this kind of distress was often relieved by a dose of paregoric. Could he supply me with some? "Nice try," he said. It turns out that the equivalent of a court order is needed to get this old remedy that was routinely given to infants in the early 1900s. You know—the generation that weathered the Great Depression, won World War II and stared the Russians down in the Cold War, etc.

Charlie "Bird" Parker, one of the greatest jazz musicians who ever picked up a sax, once observed that he paid thousands of dollars to doctors for cures that didn't work, but could pass a couple of hundred bucks to some shady character in a back alley for stuff that made him feel immediately better.

Now I'm not advocating this lifestyle. Charlie had addiction problems and died early with a number of ailments "any one of which could have killed him," stated a doctor who examined his body. I give Charlie the benefit of a doubt, though. I maintain that he might have been well intentioned and on the right path for homeopathic treatment—he just didn't get the dosage right.

Just recently, I had another brief appointment with a doctor and stomach treatment options were raised. Our session over, I asked, very carefully, if paregoric was a possibility. She gave me "that look" and I knew what was coming. As I put on my jacket and headed out the door, I heard her response behind my back. "Nice try," she said.

OFF THE BOTTOM OF MY HEAD

Mushroom Jobs

Not long ago, my wife corralled me for a simple kitchen repair.

"That sliding drawer under the sink is in terrible shape. It's rusting and it sticks."

Not a problem, thinks I. A couple of hours and we will be as good as new here. We go down to our neighborhood mega home improvement center and buy a brand new one—stainless steel—a real beauty. Back home I assemble my tools and remove the old unit. But the vinyl tiles that we have put in the bottom of the sink cabinet to resist moisture and permit easier cleanup are in bad shape. No point in installing the new unit over them. Back to MHIC for new tiles.

When the old tiles are pulled...ugh! The particle board bottom of the cabinet is rough and eroded. But wait! There is a nice piece of hardboard in the cellar and it is jigsawed into the right shape to form a new cabinet bottom. Voile! Well, almost. When it is snapped into place, the front of the cabinet pops out. OK, they are 20 years old, after all. My wife asks, "What now, handyman?"

"The old fixit remedy, Dearie—glue and screw, glue and screw."

The cabinet front is secured, the tiles are cut to fit, glued to the hardboard and finally the new sliding drawer is installed. Two days later.

You probably have examples of your own, but let me tell you my all-time favorite mushroom job. This chilling tale is absolutely true. As I often remind friends who ask me where I get my story ideas—I am not smart enough to make up stuff like this.

My friend Ted was a consummate professional with a very responsible job in a large corporation. He is not, however, the type folks call "handy." One day his wife pointed out that a few dead bugs had accumulated in the globe of the ceiling fan light in the kitchen. The little carcasses could be seen when the lamp was lit. Since he had the day off, could he kindly remove them? When Ted's wife left for work, Ted started the job.

He discovered that the fan could be reached by standing with one foot on a chair and one on the kitchen range. Why in heck haul a stepladder in from the garage? He climbed up and started to remove the globe. At some point—and details are vague on this, as Ted has never offered to clear things up—he was working like this when he stepped on one of the burners. Luckily it was not on. He smashed the ceramic socket.

Ah well. It could happen to anyone. He interrupted his work to call the appliance repairman but figured that time wasted is money spent.

So back to work, but with extra caution taken not to place a foot on any working part of the stove. So cautious, that at some point—and Ted doesn't care to discuss this either—he began to lose his balance and grabbed for the closest support, which would be one of the fan blades. Luckily it was not on. It broke, of course.

Ah well. It hadn't snapped completely off. It was still attached by some pretty substantial slivers; and what do they make Elmer's for, anyway? Ted patiently glued the dangling blade back to a horizontal position with a duct tape splint—to be removed when the glue dried. Innovation at work.

About this time the repairman showed up and replaced the stove burner element and socket. Good as new. He did, however, point out to Ted, very tactfully, that he had seen evidence of a cockroach nest in the far reaches of the stove. Ted was dismayed but not deterred. Could a pest control guy make an emergency call? He could, it turns out, and as time ticked away, he came to the house and applied the treatment to take care of the bugs.

Ted is getting just a bit nervous now. His wife will be due home before very long. He must see if his fan blade repair is a success.

The duct tape splint is removed and all evidence of any mishap is gone. To be sure, the bugs are still in the globe over the ceiling fan light. He begins working on a story about a crisis at work that had required a lengthy phone conference.

"Oh what a tangled web we weave, when first we practice

to deceive." Sir Walter Scott.

Ted was in the den, working out the details of this subterfuge, when his wife came home. She walked into the kitchen and turned on the ceiling lamp and fan to appraise her hubby's good work.

Elmer didn't hold. The jury-rigged fan blade sailed through the kitchen window.

No Rest for the Industrious

Years ago, when we went to the beach, the highest tech item packed was a pair of binoculars. When I got tired of surf and sand, I would retire to the porch of our beachfront rental and watch the beach scene. It was a joy to watch kids and grandkids splashing around, storks diving for lunch, shrimp boats lazing offshore—and the occasional dolphin.

The beach isn't just for vacation anymore. Ads for cell phones, laptops and other devices stress that you can now conduct business anywhere! Generally pictured are men and women of this brave new world contentedly negotiating big deals while the sun shines, the surf roars and seabirds wheel in the background.

New terms have entered our language—a blackberry isn't just something you remember from mama's pies. Every coffee shop and fast food eatery has a Wi-Fi sticker on the door. You are just not cutting it if you are going through life without your wireless tether to the world.

A few weeks ago, I was using the restroom in one of the large home improvement stores, when I heard one end of an animated conversation as I washed my hands. I looked around, but saw no one. The speaker was saying, "now if you drill three holes in the bottom of that template, you can line things up, and..." I suddenly realized that an employee was discussing a project on a cellphone in one of the restroom stalls! A customer service call even greater than nature's had to be dealt with.

At one time I commuted from Charlotte to a job in upstate New York. I flew up on Sunday nights and back on Friday evenings. The return trip routed through LaGuardia Airport. I was invariably on the same flights as other business folks heading home after a week's work.

I have always enjoyed flying. Sure, airports are a hassle these days, with all of the security measures, but my spirits always lift with the plane, as the wheels retract and we head to a destination—home in this case—that I am looking forward to.

On one such flight, I boarded late and the plane was nearly

full as I headed toward my seat near the back. I noticed something that I had not paid much attention to before. As I schlepped my luggage down the narrow aisle I walked past row after row of businessmen and women seated with open laptop computers. Waiting, no doubt, for the moment, when—once airborne—the pilot would give them permission to turn their machines on.

I go back far enough to remember the secretarial typing pools. They were large open office areas with rows of—always women in those days—banging noisily away to churn out the documents of a large business. They were the memos, procedures, research reports and other such paperwork that make industry hum—then and now.

I was immediately struck by how much the scene on the plane reminded me of the clattering typing pools of years before. The laptops are quieter, computer files have replaced the stacks of paper, but the product is the same.

No quiet reflection of the week's activity for these fliers. No idle meditation on the panorama of clouds around and earth far below. No relaxed scanning of magazine, paper or a valued letter. No restful nap to refresh a weary spirit or *sleep that knits up the ravelled sleave of care*, in Shakespeare's words.

The saying goes that there is no rest for the wicked. These days, there isn't much for the industrious either.

Hippy Days & Hippy Nights

A few years ago, Michael Jackson released an album called *Bad.* Not long after this, we were watching *The Doors*, with a few friends. This movie relates the story of the noted 60's rock band and their thoroughly dissolute lead man, Jim Morrison. One friend, Danny, is a Viet Nam vet. He has seen stuff he would just as soon have not. He knows bad. As we watched Jim Morrison's notorious life unravel on film, Danny remarked, "And Michael Jackson thinks *he's* bad…"

He was right. Jim Morrison both influenced, and was defined by, an era that was…ahem…interesting.

In 1969, my wife and I briefly considered going to see the Woodstock Concert, but we would have had to take a couple of days off from work, and get baby sitters for our small children. Actually, that whole scene was swirling around everywhere in those days. You didn't have to go far.

Watkins Glen, a small town in upstate New York, was a sports car racing Mecca. No slap against NASCAR, but we liked races where the cars made right turns, left turns, went up hill and down, and you could watch an open cockpit Cooper duel with a Jaguar through an S bend. There were very few grandstand seats and most folks watched the races in lawn chairs or standing at various points along the road course.

Races at The Glen were something to be experienced. A group of enterprising young men would park a big delivery truck and lounge around in lawn chairs on the top of it at a strategic location near the main gate. They had big placards with numbers on them and urged passing girls to lift up their shirts and sweaters to reveal their superstructure and receive a rating for the same.

My wife, when she went with us, ignored these blandishments (naturally), but a surprisingly large number of young women complied to see how they measured up in the eyes of the judges. My wife scoffed at most of the marks awarded, but then she would have been a good 9.5 in those days—easy for her to be less than impressed, you might say.

Nighttime brought new thrills. Exotic and suspicious

smoke, and smells of a thousand campfires would drift over the track as dusk settled over the multitudes.

There was low spot outside the track called the bog. In wet weather, it was just that, a virtual swamp that was the site of a popular ritual every year. As the evening darkened, a chant would begin near the bog. Slowly at first, from one or two voices, then picked up by dozens—then hundreds: "The bog needs a car! The bog needs a car! *The bog needs a car!*" It would grow in volume and intensity until an offering was made.

Someone would sacrifice an old junker to be burned there. As flames rose from the pyre, rock music would be blaring, and a group of young people would be dancing around. A second—even a third car—would sometime be added to the oblations.

Clothing was varied, and in some cases, optional. We saw one young man in straw hat, hiking boots and a belt holding beer cans—nothing else. He didn't strike many folks as that unusual. Nothing seemed to be too outrageous.

Sleep before the big race was almost impossible if you were camping on the grounds. The hoopla went on through most of the night. If my buddy Joe and I—two relatively staid individuals—were able to catch a little shut-eye, we awoke to incredible sights. Bleary-eyed, mud-caked, zombies wandered around in a minefield of beer cans and empty bottles. A charred old sedan, or two, still smoked in the bog. Ah, the joys of youth.

But it was race day! Joe and I would pick a particular spot on the track that promised a lot of action and watch from there. Now and then, we might move to another location as our moods and the strategies of the drivers dictated. We were not tied to any chairs but the folding ones we carried with us.

One particularly hot summer race day, a thunderstorm hit the track and people dove for whatever cover they could find. Joe and I happened to be near one of the large culverts that served as walkways under the road course. A lot of other people had the same idea and the place was jammed when Joe and I reached it. The air was blue with smoke, and it wasn't from Lucky Strikes or the Formula I cars circling the track. Now it isn't that Joe is a lot less worldly than I, but I immediately recognized an essence of the herbalist's art and cautioned my pal—"Whatever you do, don't inhale, Joe."

The Glen ran into hard times and closed down in 1980.

One particular incident was a big contributor to its decline. In 1974, a group of Brazilian fans chartered a Greyhound bus to travel to the Glen and cheer on Emerson Fittipaldi, who was tied for first place in Formula I points and needed a high finish to take his second FI Championship.

The driver unloaded his passengers and parked the unattended bus. Sometime after this, the bus was stolen by someone "with long hair and naked from the waist up," as he was described later by eyewitnesses. He circled the bog several times before driving, at high speed, into the pile of earlier sacrifices. The Greyhound was set afire and burned for hours.

The Glen gradually fell into disrepair and was in danger of dissolving, but was purchased by new owners and restored in 1984. The bog was filled in. More grandstand seating was added. The facility is much slicker and it even has a race on the NASCAR circuit.

The crowd is certainly different. I suppose a certain

percentage will consider themselves rowdies. I'm here to tell them that they—like Michael Jackson—are up against a powerful precedent.

I was there, man.

Slumbering Monsters and Hidden Heroes

Deep beneath Kroneborg Castle in Denmark, at the end of a narrow, gloomy hall, sits *Holger Danske*. Carved in stone and seated on a large stone chair, he sleeps—arms folded, chin on chest—with a broad sword across his lap, and a shield by his side. Water from the ceiling of this dank chamber drips on his Viking helmet and down his bearded face. He will awake, Danish legend holds, if the kingdom is threatened, and indeed...but more on that later.

Many cultures have a sleeping giant myth—sometimes hero, sometimes villain, and occasionally a conflicted and unpredictable entity.

Jewish folklore has many tales of the *Golem*. He is a monster shaped in clay and brought to life by the power of a holy man. Once animated, the Golem serves his creator, but he is an incomplete creation with some serious flaws.

In legend, the Golem was activated to protect a Jewish community threatened by others. The Golem cannot speak and is soulless—and thus dangerous and not able to live with humans. Once his mission is accomplished, the Golem must be deactivated by the holy man, and his dust returned to a casket to await another summons. In one tale, the Golem fell in love with a human maiden after his primary mission was accomplished. Because he was mute, he couldn't make his case to the young lady and ravaged the countryside in a rage of frustration.

The geology of Connecticut features a lot of ridges running north-south, but one unique ridge six miles north of New Haven runs east-west and has the distinctive profile of a giant form. The Native Americans in the area called the Giant *Hobbomock*.

Hobbomock has a stone canoe, and the Thimble Islands, in Long Island Sound, are his stepping-stones. Although considered a hero by the tribes in the region, he was not one to irritate. He once became angry at their neglect of him and stamped his foot near the current location of Middletown, causing the Connecticut River to change course. A good spirit cast a spell on Hobbomock causing him to sleep forever so that he would do no further damage.

Frederick I, also known as *Barbarossa*, is the subject of many sleeping hero legends. He participated in the Second Crusade, and although that expedition was a disaster, Barbarossa acquitted himself well and became an early king of Germany. He had a successful reign, but a rather ignominious death. He drowned while trying to ford the Goksu River—in full armor. Nonetheless, he is revered in legend, and is said to be sleeping in a cave with his knights, where the circling of ravens around the entrance will signal them to come to Germany's aid in a time of trouble.

But back to that old Norseman slumbering in the catacombs of Kroneborg.

Nazi Germany invaded Denmark in 1941. The Danes were overwhelmed as German tanks rolled across the flat landscape and Nazi planes controlled the skies. They quickly realized that their modest little military was badly overmatched, and resistance would result in their massacre. They surrendered.

The Nazis had other plans anyway. In Denmark, they had not only a rich bread basket, but they sensed a chance to erect a model Aryan state—a kind of testimony to the superiority of their pure-race theories.

But these sons and daughters of Vikings had their own ideas on how a state should be run, and soon the Danish Resistance Movement—the Underground—was born.

Who is to say that deep in the bottom of Kroneborg Castle

a sleeping hero did not awake? That the old stone Viking roused from his long slumber, lifted his mighty sword, settled his helmet over his stern visage, and strode into the long night of Nazi occupation.

The Danish Underground operated under the code name—and issued communiqués signed by—*Holger Danske.*

Staying at the Quaint & Cozy

Not long ago, my wife and I hosted two cousins—vintage widows from Europe—and the four of us traveled up to Pennsylvania in a rented minivan to attend a family wedding. We were eager to show our foreign relatives some authentic Americana, so my wife booked rooms in a bed and breakfast close to the wedding site. Their web page showed an impressive Victorian structure and my wife gushed on about how quaint and cozy it was.

My alarm system should have gone off. You remember the Victorian notions of comfort, don't you? This was the era that put men in high starched collars and women in whalebone corsets.

After a long and tiring drive, we pulled up in front of this turreted fortress, wedged between a fraternal lodge hall and an all-night gas station.

The parking lot was accessible from a rear alley off one of the town's streets. Once in, you were faced with two rows of cars parked on a slant. You want to go to dinner later you say? Just put that minivan in reverse and back up into, and through, that unlit alley.

But wait! What's that narrow little curbed exit at the end of the parking lot? The egress for your horse and buggy back in the days when this house was built, that's what. I found this out when I scraped the tires on both sides going through it. Once out, I pulled over to see if I would have to concoct a story for the rental agency to explain how the *Michelin* got wiped off the sidewalls.

But I am ahead of the story. After we found our parking space behind the B&B, the Innkeeper joined us as we hauled our suitcases from the van. He was 40 years my junior with a 50 pound weight advantage. An ex-footballer, no doubt.

"I'll help you with that," he grinned, and gallantly took the hand luggage from one of the ladies. I was left to schlep the rest up to the second floor of this 19th century barn to our rooms at the top of a winding, three-landing, narrow Victorian staircase.

My wife and I got a single queen-sized bed and a Biltmore-sized dresser adequate for the wardrobe of a family of four. I would gladly have traded three-fourths of it for a single easy chair and a reading lamp. Our cousins had it better. Their room came with a single rickety, straight-backed chair. I also discovered a great truth that night. There is one thing worse than sleeping in a bad bed—sleeping *two* in a bad bed. We jostled for position most of the night and I woke very early with bags under my eyes almost down to my mustache.

I learned later that the generators running the ice machine in the gas station next door serenaded our cousins in the next room as they fought for sleep that night. And we all had to get ready for a wedding coming up that afternoon.

I left this place to see what I could find while the others were still trying to rescue a bit of sleep. Miraculously, a major hotel chain had just opened a new hotel across town. As I told their staff my sad story, they put a cup of coffee in my hand, dabbed their eyes with tissues and said that they would welcome our party of four and waive the half-day's fee customarily charged for early check in. It was my turn to get all misty-eyed.

I drove back to get the rest of my platoon and we changed quarters within the hour.

Every now and then I get one of those email forwards that carry on about how much better things were back then—the music, the cars, the movies; you name it. I season that nostalgic stuff with a very big grain of salt.

Ok, I'll give you the music. Just let me have the SunnySide Suites over the House of Usher.

Chuck Thurston

The New Math for Old Students

When our children were in primary school, we were suddenly exposed to the "new math" when they asked for help on their homework. I just exchanged notes with a grandson starting high school. He said that he is taking Honors Geometry—that has an ominous ring to it—but next year he moves on to Algebra II and "other stuff." Set theory? Matrices? Modular arithmetic? I pointed out that my generation put a man on the moon and we didn't even have laptops.

But the kids we helped back then have moved on to jobs and family, as will our grandchildren in their time. We seniors manage to fill our days with happy pursuits. "When you are through learning, you are through," is a favorite saying of ours, so we find ourselves students once again, learning how to make the most of our senior years.

A lot of this focus is on trying to stay fit. It is probably the most important job that all of us have when we retire. You can do it on your own, but joining a program is more fun—and a motivator—when others are involved to help and encourage. There are a thousand fitness plans out there, but frankly, most good advice is built around a simple axiom: "Eat less, move more." That's it.

You can support this simple truth with facts and figures— you might think of this as the new math for seniors. Don't be discouraged if you were never any good in school. I have designed some simple word number problems you can work on—answers at the end of this column.

1) Your doctor tells you that your cholesterol level is 265— too high, he says, and you should lower it by 25%. What is the best method of accomplishing this?

a. attend all the church suppers you can

b. drink more diet cola

c. pray

d. ignore him; the stress of dieting is more dangerous than high cholesterol

2) You had bacon and eggs for breakfast and you plan on

having the meatloaf special at Mom's Diner tonight. You recently read an article that said you should limit your fat intake to 30% of your daily caloric intake. Is it OK for you to have a BLT for lunch?

3) You recently dusted off your treadmill and found that the slope setting the last time it was used—in 1987—was 7.5. You are 65 years old. Is this a safe setting for you to use in resuming your exercise program?

4) You understand that meaningful cardio-vascular exercise calls for a heart rate 65 to 85 percent of the maximum heart rate for your age and you purchased a heart rate monitor to track it. You are 71. You have heard that Lance Armstrong routinely exercises at 95 percent of his maximum heart rate. You decide to try it and discover that your monitor suddenly stops working. Are these devices designed to cut off at certain levels?

Don't be discouraged if you don't get a 100 on the first try. Staying healthy is a day-by-day effort for all of us. We understand the occasional temptations to skip the exercise, cheat on the diet, and ignore the good advice and the warnings. Just do the best you can.

Here are the answers:

1) If you can find a church supper without green beans boiled for three hours in country ham, fried chicken and biscuits and banana pudding—go for it! Otherwise, c is your best option.

2) Good news. You can actually have a BLT sandwich. Just eliminate the bread, bacon and mayo.

3) No. A slope of 7.5 is roughly the grade on Route 40 from Swannanoa up to Asheville. Perhaps you have noticed the runoffs for trucks with no brakes on the way down this stretch. Don't take the chance. See if you can walk back and forth to your mailbox without breathing hard first.

4. No. This problem may be graver than you think. First, see if you can fog a mirror. If this little test is inconclusive, call your doctor, but it may require an out-of-body effort.

Life Is a Package Deal

Whether you are sailing along smoothly in everyday activities or trying to navigate in turbulent waters, life has a way of unfolding things in an up or down sequence. I think that, in some philosophies, this is called your karma—and it can be good or bad. In other words, when you mess one thing up badly, it seems to set off a chain of troublesome events. And when you have a nice accomplishment it seems to set off a string of small successes.

Psychologists probably have a formal name for these sequences, but I offer you my own, with real life case studies. The downer experience is what I call *The Failure Funk*.

I once had this conversation with a young man:

He: "I am really depressed these days."

Me: "And why is that?"

He: "I just lost my third job this month!"

Me: "Good heavens, what is happening?"

He: "Too many missed days, they said."

Me: "What's the reason for that?"

He: "Well, I have this drinking problem."

Me: "Hmmmm. It wouldn't surprise me if you were depressed..."

And, as you might guess, the opposite is true. When you accomplish something really good, other successes seem to fall into place. I call this *The Triumph Track*.

Here's an example of a conversation I had with a young woman not long ago:

She: "I have decided to go for a degree at the community college!"

Me: "That's great! Any particular reason?"

She: "Well, I just got more motivated to study in the last few weeks."

Me: "What brought that on?"

She: "It's funny; I wanted to lose a few pounds so I started exercising."

Me: "...and you found yourself with more energy."

She: "Exactly. I am not so beat at the end of the day."

Me: "That's wonderful. More get-up-and go for evening classes."

She: "Yes…well, I dumped Harold, too."

You may poo-poo these patterns, but let me illustrate with an example from my life.

A few years ago, I went through a period of bad headaches. I tried all of the over-counter-stuff, which didn't help much, then finally went to see a doctor. After they had done several scans of my head, and couldn't find anything –my wife was not surprised—the doctor finally prescribed the mother of all painkillers for me. I hate to take medicine to begin with, and never a drop more than is absolutely necessary, but he set me straight.

In effect, he told me that sometimes a very strong dose of something is needed to break the cycle of—in my case—headache pain. And he was right. Once I passed through the zombie state induced by these horse pills, the headaches went away, and nowadays, I rarely have to resort to anything stronger than an occasional aspirin.

I found this theory and these patterns so compelling that I have been tempted to put a shingle out in front of my office and take on clients who want to stay on an even course in their lives.

On *The Triumph Track*? Keep it chugging! In a *"Failure Funk?"* Turn that karma around! Break out of that dive! What could be simpler?

Well, one thing comes to mind, if you can afford a plane ticket to Denmark.

In medieval times, your bad luck was often attributed to witches, and the cure for that was to burn the witches who had brewed it up for you. As society became more civil, this practice stopped—with real witches, that is.

Denmark is a land of beaches and coasts. On each June 23, people are drawn to them to celebrate St. Hans Aften —or St. John's Eve. It is the summer solstice—never completely dark in this far northern country at this time, but as the twilight settles over these long shorelines, a series of bonfires is lit up and down the coast. From any particular vantage spot, you can see them on either side of you, blazing away in the evening's dusk.

Into the flames are thrown the effigies of witches. They represent your ills and woes of the past year. People also throw slips of paper in that list the troubles they want to be done with. Up in smoke they go. And as the papers are reduced to wisps of smoke and curling ashes, the people join hands and sing:

"Vi elsker vort land... den er bunden af sommerens hjerter så varme, så glade"

"We love our country…this is the bottom of summer, our hearts so warm, so glad."

And why not, indeed? You have thrown all your cares and bothers and concerns into the fire. Up and down the long beaches, thousands of your countrymen have done the same, while holding hands and singing. The midsummer twilight breaks and the people drift away into a new dawn as the fires ebb and die.

I Can't Tell You Why

I am not usually a name dropper, since I rarely hob-nob with people whose names you would recognize, but my wife and I once had a late evening supper with the late (and great) science fiction writer, Ray Bradbury. Ray had come to town to deliver a talk and do a book signing at an author's festival, and we knew folks who knew him. Later on, my wife and I and the other couple joined him for a light salad and a glass of wine at his hotel's restaurant.

He turned out to be thoroughly genial and genuine; as pleasant a supper companion as you could hope for. At some point in his talk earlier in the evening, Ray had advised his audience to stay away from the local TV news, and we wanted to question him on this. He claimed that in the eternal hunt for viewers and market share, local news presented a wholly cynical and distorted picture of life.

Ray is probably right, but I think his observation says as much about us, as it does about the TV producers. What do we find that makes us continue to tune into this daily infusion of misery dosed with pandering speculation?

Here's an example of a typical hook to get you to come back after the commercial break: A 10 second shot of a trashed church interior is shown, and one of the anchors says—in dramatic fashion: "We'll return after the break, with an interview of Sheriff Jones about this case...you won't believe *why* the vandals caused this destruction!" (fade to antacid commercial).

I don't really care about the *why*—the obsession of our age if ever there was one. In most cases, the perps themselves couldn't tell you why. And I am not all that interested anyway. After I have seen *what* these hoodlums have done, I want to move on to *how* we are going to catch them, and *what* we will do with them *when* they are caught!

"Why" can be a dangerous word. Consider this: my neighbor's son does my yard work and I confront him with, "Jesse, *why* didn't the weeds get whipped around the mailbox?" Instantly, Jesse is on his guard. Is this an accusation? Am I being judgmental in some way?

Now, let me rephrase it: "Jesse, *what's* the story about the weeds around the mailbox?" Aha! Now Jesse is on my side! Changing the *why* to *what* sends Jesse the signal that I will accept an explanation, and that he and I can solve this little problem together. He ran out of gas, he forgot about it, he was called away to do something for his mother...who knows? And frankly, I don't care. I just want to know *when* he's going to get around to it.

And the *what's* are not without their problems, either. In many cases, people are asking the what of things that are, frankly, imponderable. "What is the meaning of existence?" comes to mind. I won't stress my brain with speculations of this sort, but my wife insists on testing me every now and then, with questions that are equally unanswerable.

"Why do you think the 1) little store down the road closed? 2) the Hamilton's are separating? 3) the price of gas keeps going up?" I can only reply—with all the sincerity I can muster—"I have no idea." This never turns out to be a satisfactory answer.

Now Ray dealt in science fiction, but true science only accepts as "proven" those things that can be confirmed by experiment. I put "proven" in quotes, because scientists themselves are loath to use this term. Their take is that you can only show that something is false—and, therefore, by definition, its correlate must be...well...true.

That is, it's true until you accept something that makes more sense. I once heard a devout Christian and a committed Atheist argue about proof that God exists. Heck, we can't prove that two plus two equals four. We treat that as an acceptable hypothesis, however, because whenever we have used it to balance a checkbook, build a bridge or send men to the moon—it has worked. In other words, nobody has come up with a better resultant than four, for 2 + 2.

For all the ancients knew, the earth was flat and the moon was made of green cheese. Observation of the night sky and the vast rolling ocean from where you were sheep herding could lead to both of these conclusions. Explorers of planet and space have proved the falsity of these early conclusions—and left yet more questions to be answered.

The great philosopher, Montaigne, had this motto emblazoned on the ceiling of his library: Que sçais-je? *What do I know?* Legend has it that, when he was dying, he had himself wheeled into this room and—with trembling finger—pointed toward this motto overhead...before breathing his last.

Now look—if this was the final conclusion reached by one of the greatest minds in history, how in the world am I supposed to know the things asked of me by my wife?

I have enough trouble trying to figure out the rationale behind other great puzzles:

"Why don't fire ants and yellow jackets fight each other to the death?"

"What do they plant to get seedless watermelons?"

"How can you tell if Limburger cheese has gone bad?"

And—if your parents couldn't stand your music, and you can't stand that of your kids'—and your kids are disgusted with your grandchildren's—when was music ever any good?

Answer these, my friends, and you have performed a real service for me.

Incidentally, on the drive home after our evening with Ray Bradbury, my wife remarked, "What a charming man!" Frankly, after viewing the inscription he wrote in the book he autographed for her, a lesser man than I would have asked him to step outside. But, understanding and sophisticated as I am—and even though my wife is thoroughly charming—I was still about to ask *why* she thought...*OOPS!!* Rephrase alert!

"Yes, you are right dear. *What* is it about him that folks find so appealing?" And I might have added, under my breath, "...and *how* do I get some of it?"

LIFE IN THE SLOW LANE

The Women in My Life

I have heard friends and acquaintances say over the years "Oh—your poor mother!" It wasn't prompted by any history of abuse or neglect. She was simply outnumbered. Mom was the only female in our household. My four brothers and our Dad constituted a clear gender majority. I never attached any significance to this fact in my boyhood.

A couple of years ago, my doctor of many years told me at one of my visits, that he was retiring. "You will have to get another doctor," he said. This is always a speed bump in one's life. I told him I would give it some thought.

Shortly afterwards, his clinic posted a picture in the lobby. It was a newly minted physician—an attractive blonde woman, which, of course, was a draw. I have never been one to let looks trump utility, though. I had been a manager, after all—and in IBM, at that. You remember the old IBM, right? Blue suits? Sincere ties? Her utility was that her personal interests were in homeopathic and geriatric medicine! This was just the person to help make these my happy years! I signed up with her right away. I had a couple of checkups that went very well, but there was a little gnawing anxiety that I couldn't get rid of. We had not broached the subject of my annual prostate exam and the time was approaching.

Now I already had a female dermatologist, and I confess that I actually looked forward to visits with her, when she would run her soft hands over my body looking for the ravages of sun and environment.

But this was different. I was barely tolerant of this check up from an older male doctor, but a young woman? On the appointed day, she ran through what she normally did and I thought that perhaps she was no more anxious to get at this little invasive procedure than I was. I knew that it was something I needed to have done, though, and I mumbled something like, "Uh...Doctor K used to...about this time...uh..."

She gave me an amused but business-like smile as she snapped on a pair of latex gloves. "Oh, don't you worry," she said.

Not many secrets left now.

Just a few weeks ago, my wife came back from a visit to our eye doctor. "You are just going to love the new doctor there," she said. I am sure I don't have to tell you the rest of this story. I made an appointment to see her the next month.

Why not? A lady has barbered my hair for many years. My Tai Chi instructor is a gal. I chat with the mail delivery lady at the mailbox now and then. My pharmacy has a covey of young ladies. I could go on and on, but let me tell you a tale from very early in the game.

When I left the military and began working in corporate America, I put my service-acquired skills to work as an electronics technician. I liked the work and I was passably good, but I knew I would find my level in this field sooner or later—and it wouldn't be all that high up.

I began attending night classes at a local college and started thinking about where I wanted to go. I was, frankly, clueless. I had a young wife, young children and I was vaguely troubled that I would someday be dead-ended on my current career path.

College night classes are a mixed bag of daytime employees, students making up classes, retirees learning for learning's sake, and hopeful career changers such as myself. I started out with the courses required in any program. I could always settle on a major later.

I waffled through a couple of subjects, liked them, and signed up for a course in American Literature. The teacher was Doctor T—one of the straightest shooting gals I ever met. When you get into 20th century writing you get into some pretty explicit stuff. One reviewer at the time said of Henry Miller's *Tropic of Cancer*, "This isn't a book—this is a sewer!"

And Dr. T called an organ an organ.

One Sunday I worked on a paper for her class as I watched a pro football game. I don't know why I remember this, but the Washington Redskins were playing someone. I don't even recall the topic of the paper I was writing. It was an analysis of some piece of literature or another. I had one eye on the game, likely a can of beer—or two—in front of me, and I dashed off a paper that I felt should be good enough. My good marks to this point had made me a little cocky. I could ace this stuff half in the bag.

I turned it in on Monday and waited for the next class to get her comments on my masterpiece. I got nothing from her until the class was breaking up for the night, and she asked me to stay afterwards. As I sat alone in the room, she approached my desk and threw the paper down in front of me. "This is crap!" she said—although she didn't say crap—she used the barracks vernacular. Rhymes with "spit" if you're wondering. I glanced down at the scattered sheets on my desk and noted that she had written almost as much in the margins as I had in the essay itself.

Then I got the verbal readout. I wish I had a recording of this. I'd play it any time in my life I was tempted to dog it on a project. I'd play it for kids and grandkids. I'd put it on a sound truck and run it through farmyards and neighborhoods that are dealing with this problem or that.

I'd make politicians memorize it.

Basically, she said that I should be ashamed of myself -that I was squandering my talent and wasting her time; that there were other folks in her class perhaps with less aptitude for the subject than I, but who worked for everything they got while I piddled around doing no more than absolutely necessary to cruise through. My paper essentially insulted her.

That episode turned my fledgling college career around. I took every class Dr. T taught after that, and worked like a dog to regain her favor. I owe her a lot.

I owe a lot to all of the women in my life.

So here's to them. Here's to Drs. Deanna and Sue and Sonnie and Elizabeth. Here's to Diane and Susan and all the rest. You know who you are.

Pennies from Heaven

One summer, a neighboring farmer a quarter mile down the road from our farm decided his well wasn't flowing fast enough and threw a stick of dynamite down it. Some folks might consider this over-kill—and what was a chicken farmer doing with dynamite anyway?

Our own farm had an artesian well—a free flowing well that is created when groundwater in a confined aquifer is pushed out to the surface under pressure. No need for a pump at the surface or hundreds of feet down. Just attach a spigot at the wellhead and turn it on when you need the water.

At any rate, our well dried up within minutes of the explosion down the road, and my dad had to drill a new one in another location. We got water at a hundred feet or so, but it had to be pumped up. No more free hydraulics.

That was our own local water conflict, but similar hassles are going on all over the globe.

Arizona and Colorado are fighting over the Colorado River—the mighty stream that carved the Grand Canyon. As it is, very little of this proud river ever reaches the ocean. It is sucked dry for irrigation and other purposes long before it gets there.

The World Bank reports that, on a global scale, eighty countries now have water shortages that threaten health and economies, while forty percent of the world—more than 2 billion people—have no access to clean water or sanitation.

North Carolina has its own not-so-small version of a water war. Eleven counties, ten cities, three Marine Commissions, the South Carolina General Assembly and the Governors of two states have at one time or another been squabbling over the Concord-Kannapolis IBT, the Inter-Basin Transfer of water from the Catawba River by cross-country pipeline to Concord and Kannapolis for the water needs of the rapidly expanding residential and commercial growth of those two cities.

When we built our cabin we decided to install a system that I had been researching for some time—rain catchment. There was no spring source on our chunk of land and the wells on that particular mountain were notoriously unreliable. A bit further up the hill from us, a property owner had drilled down over 1100 feet—and come up empty. That's an expensive hole, folks.

Rain catchment, simply described, means you catch the rain that comes off your roof gutters and pipe it to a storage cistern. You pump it out, put it through a few filters and there you have it. How much you get depends on your roof size and the amount of rain—an inch of rain on the roof of my little 24 X 32 cabin gives me around 430 gallons. How safe? Let's just say I'll match my water sample against any spring or drilled well source any day. The Wilkes County health department is just fine with it.

After our experiences, I wondered why more businesses didn't take advantage of these systems. The big box stores, with their huge roof areas, would seem to be ideal candidates. Perhaps the slower influx of customers in rainy weather could be countered by the free water and reduced dependence on city and town supplies. Looking hopefully at the gray skies might be the new paradigm for the storeowner.

We were never as appreciative and watchful of rain as we have been since we installed our own system. We watch the TV weather as closely as any farmer to see if the radar patterns show showers drifting over our little corner of the county. "Pennies from Heaven" we call them.

Sometimes I feel as if I should share this wonderful discovery with others.

I will, by golly.

"Ms. Secretary, get this memo to the North Carolina Research Campus in Kannapolis: "

Sir/Madam: Given the current water woes of your fair city, you might consider designing the 350-acre complex you are now constructing to yield an unexpected bonus. I don't know how much water you can expect to get out of a measly pipeline running across a couple of counties—or how much you'll pay for it—but if only 100 acres of your magnificent project are equipped to catch rain, any old summer afternoon thunder-boomer that delivers a piddling little inch of rain will furnish you with around (...umm...square feet per acre...multiply the rainfall...factor the .6233...whoa!) 2.5 million gallons of water! Boy, that's a lot of toilet flushes!

Think about it.

You're welcome.

Comforting the Afflicted

When we part with friends after a visit these days, we throw in a "take care of yourselves, now," along with the hugs and handshakes. And we mean it.

A couple of years ago, and in the space of four months, three of our cohorts—all of a certain maturity—suffered falls. And suffered is the right word.

A graceful ballet instructor friend kicked things off with an unplanned pirouette over spilled detergent in her laundry room. She said later that she didn't recall slipping—just a brief moment when she was completely airborne. She broke her right femur, the biggest bone in the body, in what was surely one of the cruelest accidents a dancer could have. Rather like a watchmaker breaking a thumb.

A month later, a Danish cousin slipped on the ice in (where else?) Iceland, and broke a bone in her foot. She praised the Icelandic health care system and graduated from walker, to cane, to a painful hobble over time, but in her last report said that her foot was still swollen and sore after a long day. She is a teacher—yet another injustice.

Skip two months. A good friend missed the last rung while descending a stepladder. He required a hip replacement to repair the damage—never a routine procedure. This fellow recently retired and looked forward to a lot of those handyman jobs that he does better than he could hire to have done. He is not the type to tolerate merely adequate workmanship.

All three of these folks had to put important functions in their life on hold for a while but are now back in the game of life, I am happy to say. Let me offer a few pieces of advice to my cohorts—whether you just want to avoid a mishap of your own, or are taking care of another who has had one.

First: I am never going to tell a senior to slow down. I have no intention of doing that myself in the sense that I stop doing the things I like or ought to do—but I am going to be more deliberate as I go about them. Sometimes we forget that we don't have quite the reflexes, reaction times or hand-eye coordination that we did in our younger days. Our depth perception is perhaps not what it once was. We have lost a beat or two in the dance of life. Don't stop dancing, for heaven's sake—just mind the step. Look for that happy medium between frenzied activity and walking around on eggshells.

Second: If your own circle of friends includes someone who is laid up from an accident like this, pay them a visit, and come prepared. Too often we stop by to see someone recuperating out of a sense of obligation or spiritual duty—and there's nothing wrong with that, but throw in a little extra. Instead of twiddling your thumbs and checking the clock to see when you've spent an obligatory half-hour, be the best cheerleader you can be, because they will need it.

Any accident that is temporarily disabling to us seniors is a serious hit to our morale. Our pals will all regain full function at some point, but it helps them to hear it, and to look forward to returning to enjoyable pursuits. If a friend is a golfer, take him or her a golf magazine.

It is hard for a convalescent to see any good coming out of an accident, but there might be a silk purse here somewhere. Are they history buffs, or do they dabble in art? Consider bringing them books on their favorite topics or drawing and painting materials. It beats lying around and feeling sorry for themselves.

Here's the last piece of advice:

You might find yourself as a primary caretaker for a person who is laid up—perhaps for a very long time. You are very apt to go through spells when you resent your obligation and wish you had more freedom to pursue other activities. This is probably a fairly common reaction, but it is also a trap. It can load you up with resentment, guilt, feelings of inadequacy, isolation from your other life—whatever that may be. You become, in effect, a kind of mirror to the one you are caring for—another invalid, in a way.

This situation might be further complicated if the invalid is beginning "that journey from whence no man returns," as Shakespeare put it. The chances are you both know it. I can't give you much advice on handling this. Books have been written on caring for the terminally ill, and my advice would be to consult one. Everyone in this situation handles it differently.

Your patient may be bitter, resigned—perhaps even happily anticipatory to be relieved of what has probably become burdensome to them. They might get quite philosophical.

There is a story told of Jack Kelly on his deathbed. Kelly was one of 10 children in a poor Irish immigrant family, and began life as a bricklayer. He went on to gain fame and fortune. He was the father of the prominent actress—Grace Kelly.

As his family gathered around for what would be his final farewell, he chided them for their weeping and reminded them of his life. He had risen from poverty to start his own construction company and became a millionaire. He was an incredible athlete.

He was 12-0 in a military heavyweight boxing tournament until he broke an ankle. Years later he would remind the eventual champion, Gene Tunney, how lucky he—Tunney, later to become the world's heavyweight champion—was not to have faced him.

He won three Olympic gold medals in rowing.

He ran for mayor of Philadelphia and narrowly lost. President Franklin Roosevelt appointed him National Physical Fitness Director during WWII.

Jack had run well in the race of life and he knew it. The finish line held no terrors for him.

"And besides," he consoled his grieving family and friends, "I'm rather curious."

Take care of yourselves…hear?

Pond Life

As we gobbled down our lunch, my mother used to warn my brothers and me that "You'll get cramps and drown if you go swimming right after you eat!"

Good advice, perhaps, but likely wasted on us. Our peanut butter sandwiches had probably distributed themselves throughout our hyperactive systems in the 15 or 20 minutes it took us to get ready for a summer afternoon swim. Getting ready didn't involve any more than putting on cut-off jeans swim trunks and hiking up to the small pond on a hill above our farm house.

The pond was bulldozed out below a spring that had evidently been known to travelers well before us. Whatever its history, it fed our swimming hole, although our efforts barely qualified as swimming.

The pond was not very large—perhaps 10 yards across at its widest—and not very deep. Two or three strokes could propel a swimmer from one side to the other. It was not even absolutely necessary to expend your energy this way, since you could wade across if you wished. When our dad had it excavated, he kept the water level at around 4 feet.

We built a raft of sorts to paddle across it—a short voyage by any measure, but we never seemed to make it. Our raft was an old door. We had added boards as gunwales around it and caulked the seams with clay. Although we paddled mightily, it would slowly sink beneath us just a few strokes from shore.

We had devised all manner of water sports and entertainments. Swimming lessons were an early favorite, and our household pets were the pupils. The educational process simply involved throwing them in. Could dogs swim? Not a problem. Pretty well, too, although some breeds—shepherds, for instance—had to be coerced. Beagles, on the other hand, often jumped in of their own volition and frolicked with us. It was not unusual to be doggy paddling around and have a smiling hound pull alongside.

Cats were another matter. They could swim ok, but one lesson generally sufficed. After that, they ran away—soaked and bedraggled—and were tough to catch for additional experiments. Fortunately, most farms had plenty of barn cats to keep the rodent population down, so there were usually a few who were ignorant—and therefore unwary—of this tutoring. These were fair game for further testing.

The pond got a lot of company when not put to our use. We frequently saw the tracks of deer, foxes, raccoons and assorted small critters on the pond banks. The usual compliment of frogs, toads, salamanders, minnows, water snakes, mosquitoes, dragon flies, gnats and other wildlife filled out this little niche of the biosphere.

The pond had a mud bottom and five or ten minutes of activity turned it into a murky mess, and absolutely useless for bathing. I don't recall that it ever totally cleared up during the years of our usage. An occasional cow also visited the pond. These animals often, in the hottest days of the summer, waded in and stood there, and...need I say more? We now and then had to shoo one away to gain access to our pool. After an afternoon of play, our mother made us hose each other down with a garden hose before we were fit to shuck our trunks and come inside to get dressed.

Fun continued long after summer was done and the leaves had fallen. Although the spring continued to trickle up from its source, the pond froze over solid during the cold Pennsylvania winters. We all had clamp-on ice skates, and played a primitive sort of ice hockey. We had no idea of the rules of this game. Knocking a puck into a goal with a stick pretty much defined our knowledge of the sport. Our first equipment consisted of sticks and smooth, flat stones, but at some point, our Christmas wishes for hockey sticks and a genuine rubber puck were granted, and we played in real style.

The pond went through many lives. Reeds and water plants invaded it from time to time and created a swamp useless for paddling around. It silted up and had to be dredged out now and then. During long summer droughts, it dried up into a large puddle.

The pond is still there. My brother has fenced off all but a small part of the shallow end to give cows some drinking access. A large stand of oak, 2-3 feet in diameter now surround the site. I once took a botany class that described the evolution of a climax forest and this seems to be the case here. In the midst of this vegetation, the spring seeps up from its depths to feed the pond.

We found genuine arrowheads in its vicinity. Had hunters—with their spears and bows stopped there to refresh themselves? Had they dug out the heavy blue clay for their pottery?

One senses that there will be other lives awaiting this small rising aquifer. Someone may log off the grove of oaks to harvest the timber. The oaks might return. The pond may revert to swamp, or be dug out for another pond in the future. Someone can return the land to pasture and livestock will once again wade in it. It may be fenced off or opened up. Children might splash in it once more.

The ancient spring has never quit. It was an oasis for the weary hunter and the thirsty deer. Later it was the water source for the colonial farmer and his stock. Later still, it filled the swimming hole of whooping farm boys. It is there today, burbling out of the ground just as it must have in the days of the fierce Andastes—long before our history of the New World began. The ghosts of centuries hover above the murmuring trickle.

When You're Through Learning

Many folks about my age refer to themselves as "getting older." Well, that is true from the day we are born. I prefer to think of it as maturing, myself. Some people pooh-pooh this approach and make statements like, "hey, age is just a number." Wrong. Age is age, but there are a lot of different ways you can look at it. My wife has an even better expression. She says we are "getting seasoned." Very well-seasoned, I might add. Looked at this way, it suggests that we can add spice to getting older.

I was in the office of the training manager of a textile mill a few years back. As we chatted, I noticed a sign hanging on his wall: "When you're through learning...you're through." I was struck by this and told him so. "I wish I could claim credit for making it up," he said, "but I saw it on the office of another training director a while back, and I appropriated it for myself!"

"Consider it re-appropriated," I replied, and copied it down on a piece of paper to take with me. I don't know how he or his company is doing these days, but if they are in the same boat as most American textile manufacturers, he is probably following this maxim. A lot of us seniors should too.

New learning can be the seasoning—the salt, pepper and other spices—of our maturing years. Many colleges and universities allow seniors to take classes for free, or at discount. You don't have to be working toward a degree, and if you are not working for a grade, you don't have to take exams, write papers, or burn the midnight kilowatts doing readings.

This past fall, my wife and I sat in on a class in Art Appreciation at the local community college. We were easily the geezer contingent. The instructor was a young, vivacious woman, knowledgeable and enthusiastic about her topic. Our younger classmates tolerated us well and we stuck our oar into discussions when we thought we had something to contribute. It is a rare day when my wife has nothing to add, so class participation rowed merrily along.

We began the semester with a look at the cave paintings, paused with the Classicists and dived right into the Neo-Classical. We floundered there for a bit until the Romantics and Realists came along. All stuff we could understand. We marveled over the Impressionists, but recognized that things were starting to get a little fuzzy. We puzzled over the Expressionists and Surrealists—and frankly scratched our heads over the Dadaists.

Then things got really crazy. Pollock and Warhol appeared, the Minimalists started cranking out things that wouldn't challenge your average high school shop class, and people began painting their bodies and rolling around on the floor. We loved it all—even the things we didn't understand. We added quite a bit of spice to our own intellectual stew.

We made field trips to galleries and exhibits. A return visit to a museum we had wandered through many times before provided new perspectives. We will never look at art the same way again.

Physiologists say that we are capable of learning almost up until we are...ahem...planted. It takes a little longer, sometimes. We may have to re-read that passage another time or two; we won't master a motor skill—a dance step or a Tai Chi move—without a bit more practice. But learn we can, because we must, for—when we are through learning...we are through.

I'm not through. That college's spring catalog has something called Environmental Biology. Hmmm. "ecological concepts, population growth, natural resources, environmental problems..."

Sign me up.

Check Your Brain

We have a grandson with Asperger's Syndrome—a variant of autism. He certainly has a different view of the world, but a highly realistic one for all that.

One of the local television stations used to have a channel that ran nothing but feeds from the weather radar. A mechanical voice would intone the forecasts and other useful meteorological messages. Dallas was mesmerized by it and would watch it by the hour. I was doing something in the kitchen one time, as the weather outside began to threaten rain. Dallas came running in to give me the latest: "Grandpa! Grandpa! Large hail and damaging winds!"

I had to admit—this was news we could really use. We went out to the deck immediately and stowed the chairs.

Not long ago, I had a small growth taken off my neck and walked around with a bandage for a few days. Dallas was curious about it, and I figured this was a teachable moment to introduce the concept of surgery, so I told him a bit about the procedure. Shortly after that, we drove him to one of his periodic psychological development evaluations, and I decided to chide him a bit. I asked, "Are you going to see the doctor for some kind of surgery?"

"Nah," he replied, matter-of-factly, "They're just gonna check my brain."

Indeed.

I had an uncle who used to characterize himself as having a "strong back and a weak mind." I will attest to the strong back part. He had no more than a 5th or 6th grade education, and worked as a laborer all his life: lumberjacking, dairying, plowing, planting—no life of leisure. He was, however, a font of farm and outdoor knowledge. I think he sold himself short in the brain department.

Technically, I suppose he was ignorant, but that term is often badly used. It merely means uneducated and doesn't imply stupidity. We are all ignorant of one thing or another. Don't ask me to remove an appendix, if you want to see ignorance in action.

But a brain check didn't seem like such a bad idea, and my wife and I signed up for just such a process. A laboratory in the North Carolina Research Center in Kannapolis, wants to know if blueberries can improve short-term memory function. I know mine isn't what it used to be, but I take the position that what I don't know probably won't hurt me. This might be the W. C. Fields reality denial syndrome. A doctor once told Fields that if he didn't stop his heavy drinking, his hearing was almost certainly going to be impaired. Fields wasn't worried. "The things I have been drinking, are a lot better than the things I have been hearing," he responded.

My wife, though, is downright concerned about her memory, and she has her own metaphor for it.

"Think of your brain as a big filing cabinet," she says. "As you get older, you put more and more things in it. You have grandchildren's birthdays, you accumulate more things, and must remember where you put them...it goes on and on. Before long, those drawers are filled up! If you want to locate something you have to go through file after file. Sometimes you lose your train of thought while you're checking folders! You ask yourself, what in the world was I looking for?"

Perhaps what the blueberries are meant to do is give you a better index. For instance, do I file a certain piece of info under *grandchildren* or *birthdays*—or do I keep a separate file for *Dallas*?

At any rate, the laboratory researchers are collecting their test subjects. My wife and I took a battery of tests administered by one of the brain checkers. It was an interesting procedure. We answered some questions, recalled strings of numbers and identified some pictures. We did an evaluation of our own memory capabilities, and then were asked to do the same for our spouse! It seems that if Uncle Pete starts to treat his hemorrhoids with Aqua Fresh, and brush his teeth with Preparation H—Aunt Dory will probably be the first to know! We each serve as the test strip for the other!

This research project will be conducted with several test groups over several years' time. They were still looking for test participants, the last I knew, so if you want to get your own brain checked, give the NCRC a call. When the research subjects for a particular group are selected and set to go, the researchers will give some a blueberry extract and some will get a placebo.

Periodically, over the period of the study, a cap of sensors will be placed on your head and you will be given various little computer exercises to perform. The sensors pick up what is happening, brain-wise as you push the buttons in response to computer pictures. I have a lovely multi-color picture of my brain waves in action. I am thinking of framing it and hanging it next to my college diploma.

At the completion of all the checking and data gathering, the same battery of tests that were given in the beginning, were administered again. Had we gotten worse...improved...stayed the same? We're not telling. All I'm saying is that I have a lovely multi-color pattern of my brain waves if you want to drop by and take a look.

I knew it wouldn't serve science to rig the test, but I was tempted to bribe somebody to give my wife the blueberries. My own ignorance seems blissful enough. I will keep you updated on the progress of this research...if it doesn't slip my mind.

A Hot Time in the Old Tub

The Saturday night bath is not mere legend. It was a regular part of my early childhood. The hot water heater wasn't powerful enough to deliver really hot water over the miles of cold lead pipes in the old farmhouse on a winter's night, so a big kettle was put on the wood stove and the hot water added to the tub. You tested it with a toe before committing the rest of your body to it.

Bathing was a little easier in the summer. We spent a good deal of our time in one of the farm ponds, once chores were done. We would paddle around on homemade rafts or much patched inner tubes. Usually alongside a hound or two. They seemed to have as much fun as we did. Though it rarely improved their smell, our mother seemed satisfied that the dip made us boys passably clean.

I knew that showers existed. I saw them in the movies, after all, but they weren't part of my early experience, unless I count the time I fell into—there is no other way to put it—a cow flop. It was a really fresh one, too. If you must know the details, it was afternoon recess at our small country school, and we were playing in a pasture that abutted the schoolyard. You'd think a country boy would know better.

I walked a mile under the late spring sun over dirt roads back to our farm—increasingly stiff-legged as the glop thickened and congealed on my clothing. When I got home, my mother took one look at me, and got out the farm equivalent of a shower. She washed me down with a garden hose—clothes and all—in the backyard. When I had peeled off my sodden clothes, I stood naked as a jaybird while she continued to ply the hose to make sure all traces of my mishap were removed before I could come in the house.

I had a more formal introduction to showers when I reached high school and finally found out what the locker room, that inner sanctum of the jocks, was all about. Lockers, to be sure—but showers! I had never known such luxury! I wasn't much of an athlete and only got to experience this indulgence after our Phys Ed classes. To think that this facility was designed primarily for a few elites to use simply because they could dribble a basketball or knock people down on a gridiron seemed underutilization of the rankest kind to me—not to mention the injustice of it all.

Ahh...but I made up for this shortfall. Came the military, and I discovered that showers were not only available, but using them was almost compulsory! Barracks living was close quartered, to say the least, and those who weren't very attentive to their personal hygiene, were soon reminded by shipmates to clean up their act—or else.

Now, it seems, more and more people are returning to tubs—hot tubs! And they are social venues! Friends who have installed one have told us to "bring your swim suits and head on over! You won't believe how relaxing it is!"

Hah—I will tell you about relaxing—and in good company, too. For, while in the service of our country, I also discovered the therapeutic value of showers.

On more than one return from a night on the town, we would stumble back to the base in sorry shape and head for the shower room—a long rectangular room with 10-12 shower heads around the walls. There three or four of us would adjust the water under our own showerheads to a comfortable temperature for personal use, and then turn up all the other unoccupied showers as hot as they would go.

The room would soon become thick with steam. We would bask in this environment for 20 or 30 minutes, discussing the disreputable adventures of the evening while we sweated out the toxins accumulated during these episodes. Thus purged, we would hit our bunks for a good night's sleep and be ready for muster in the morning.

Energy and resource conservation prohibit such an extravagance these days, but there may be hope. I have been reading up on saunas lately. There are some models—Finnish, I believe—where water is poured over hot stones once the little room is brought up to Saharan levels. There is soft lighting, the benches are made of teak, they can pipe in music—and some models seat three or four! Bring your towels!

It Was a Tough Job, But Somebody, etc., etc.

Every summer at the US Coast Guard Air Station in Brooklyn, NY, we were subjected to one of the most insidious summer job tortures ever devised. We had to teach a lot of beautiful young women in skimpy bathing suits how to…but let me explain.

Back in the 1950's, the overseas air carriers—Pan Am, TWA, Lufthansa, KLM, etc., had a requirement that their stewardesses get what was called "ditch drill training." On a given summer weekday, a squadron of twenty or so of these girls would show up at our base with their little duffel bags. Most work on the flight line slowed to a crawl as they were escorted into the officer's quarters. There were no facilities for female military personnel in those days, and God forbid they did their quick-change in the enlisted men's barracks.

I am not a sexist. I have a wife, daughter and four lovely granddaughters who can be appropriately strong willed—with my blessing—when the situation calls for it. On my plane trips, I am fine with a nice, gray haired, motherly flight attendant, who helps me stow my overhead luggage, takes care of my drink order and otherwise makes the journey pleasant. The overseas airlines, however, didn't think that way in the '50's. This was the era when U.S. airline regulation set the routes and fares and the airlines competed on other things—baggage handling, inflight meals, complimentary peanuts, and—I blush to say it—attractive young stewardesses. Watch the *Airport* series of films, if you think I am pulling your leg. I talked to a woman who had been a Pan Am stewardess, and she said that women exceeding a svelte weight limit were told to fix it.

These airlines also had a requirement that the "Stews," as we called them—and as they called themselves—be bilingual. That eliminated most American girls in favor of European, since the latter learn English in school to complement their native language. In our case, it meant that most of these girls were Belgian, German, Dutch or Scandinavian. It was a largely blonde, blue-eyed contingent, with a few other exotic types thrown in for variety.

But this gets better. Up until relatively recent times, European beachwear was always a lot more daring than here in the land of the Puritans. Bob Hope once remarked that when summer finally arrived, he discovered what girls had been doing all winter: "Growing skin!" In Europe, skin was in. I know that I speak for myself—and probably for most of my shipmates—when I say that we had never seen displays such as this.

We parked a couple of 40-foot patrol boats a few hundred feet off the end of the seaplane ramp as an emergency standby, and to keep rubber necks from sailing in too close. Then into the water our girls went. Now this was not all fun and games. These gals were being shown how to handle things if they ever had to ditch at sea. They learned the best methods of getting people in life jackets, exiting their aircraft, inflating life rafts and then getting people in the water into the rafts. In rare cases, perhaps getting someone in the raft back in the water. They were introduced to the Very Pistol. This was a flare gun to summon their Coastie heroes—us—if that ever became necessary.

At the end of the day, the stews would troop back into the officers' quarters to get out of their wet scanties and into their street clothes—still visions to us, by the way. Their transportation would pull up; they would board and be off.

Life at the base would return to normal, and the men would go back to their work—perhaps with a fresh set of daydreams.

A little footnote: I met my wife-to-be as a consequence of one of these training sessions. But that is a whole other story.

Lost in Space

I lived out of a locker for four years in the military, and did quite well.

Whenever I had to move from one duty station to another, I'd put on my dress blues—or whites, as the season demanded—and pack my travel orders and a few essentials in a ditty bag. I traveled light. A shaving kit, some clean skivvies and socks made up my luggage, and off I'd go. My sea bag, containing the rest of my gear, went by rail freight—in those days before UPS and FedEx.

During one move, my bag didn't make it. A new duty station, new locker, new bunk, new shipmates—and no sea bag. I borrowed what I immediately needed, bought a few items from ship's stores, and gradually replaced the stuff I had lost. I gave up checking on it after a few weeks and essentially forgot about it.

And then one day—months later, out of the blue—I got a phone call from the local train station telling me I was to pick up an item belonging to me. I didn't immediately guess what it might be, but when I was shown into the cavernous depot luggage room, there it was—dirty and scuffed beyond belief. Luggage tags and tickets from all manner of strange locations were affixed to it. My sea bag had apparently done more traveling—and perhaps had more fun—than I had in the intervening months since we were last acquainted.

I had to find room in my locker to house not only the bag's contents, but also the stuff I'd had to duplicate in its absence.

Many years later, friends arriving from Denmark discovered that one of their key pieces of luggage didn't deplane with them. This was doubly disappointing because it was Christmas time and many of the gifts they were bringing with them were in it. Weeks later it was discovered—in Istanbul! How? Why? Where might it have gone? What had it seen? Might it have been routed through the Kasbah? Had strange hands pawed through it? Might there be traces of exotic spices on it?

I thought of a phrase from Scott's last entry in his Antarctic journal—"What a tale we could have told...!" Sadly, Scott didn't survive his ordeal, but our friend's luggage eventually caught up to them, as earlier, my bag and its contents did to me.

My wife and I lived in a little apartment—converted from a garage—during the last few months of my military service. We had a phone booth bathroom, a miniature kitchenette, and another room for everything else.

When I was discharged, I watched from the front door as a large moving van pulled up to haul off our belongings. I looked it over carefully and determined that it was probably big enough to do the job. The two haulers worked quickly and efficiently. They even emptied the last of a bottle of scotch—into themselves—after warning me it was illegal to ship an open bottle of booze with my other household items. They soon had boxes of our dishes, books and assorted knick-knacks packed. They hauled off our convertible sofa, dinette set, easy chair and a few side tables, and I was looking at a barren apartment.

Before they drove off, I went out to peer into the back of the van. It was one of the most humbling experiences of my life. At first I thought that the van was empty. We were apparently the first pickup of the day, and I finally spotted, in a far dark corner near the front—it seemed a football field away—a tiny collection of stacked items that I realized was ours. Perhaps 20 cubic feet represented all we owned—outside of each other, the clothes on our backs and the few items we had put in suitcases for our move.

Over the years we accumulated more furniture, clothes and knick-knacks and moved a couple more times. In each case we upgraded to larger quarters, and we felt obligated to acquire stuff necessary to fill it. This was surprisingly easy, since every life event seemed to make a contribution.

Children married and divorced and we became custodians of things that didn't fit into their futures. Even a couple of dogs wound up in our care. Deaths in the family provided us with boxes of old treasures. Grandchildren came and we now had their artwork to add to the preserved efforts of their parents.

Boxes began filling up and storage shelves were added to accommodate them. We began having trouble finding things that we knew had to be somewhere.

Like my old sea bag and the Istanbul luggage, they were lost in space—somewhere overlooked, mislabeled, forgotten. In the attic or cellar? Had we looked in the storage shed? Perhaps lent to a relative or friend? Surely we hadn't trashed it, or given it to Goodwill...or had we?

In one instance we opened a curious box and found things that we had never unpacked from a move some years before! We had apparently never missed these items enough to launch a diligent search for them.

I don't know what this says about us. It is certain that we can do without a lot of the stuff we accumulate. Materialism and consumerism get a lot of bad press, much of it deserved, but that is not always the driver behind our accumulations.

Although we bought the child's first dancing shoes, we didn't buy her first kindergarten crayoned effort. We didn't pick up Aunt Mary's prize-winning quilt at some department store, and we can't make ourselves throw away the collar that our beloved Max wore for so many years. What are we to do with these things?

If there is a lesson here somewhere, I have not yet learned it.

Chuck Thurston

Down to the Crick

I recently got a Facebook post from one of our friends, a day after our annual church picnic:

"After the picnic Sunday, Drake and I played in the creek with Rosie and Amelia. I haven't done that since I was a kid. We found crayfish, some eggs we could see the eyeballs of whatever they were going to hatch out as, a golf ball, and metal parts from a car or tractor."

Does that paint a mental image from your childhood? It certainly took me back. We lived on a farm that had a sizeable creek running through it. In my mother's West Virginal vernacular it was a "crick," and that's what it was to us, as young boys.

On any given summer day—after morning chores were taken care of—we'd respond to Mom's question, "Where are you headed for?" with "Down to the crick!" She didn't seem to fret about any great hazard associated with this expedition, and waved us away, if our work was done.

The crick was a source of endless fun. It passed under the two lane blacktop just a few hundred yards east of our house; we owned land on both sides of the road. On the downstream side of the bridge was what we called the "deep hole." It was perhaps four feet deep and contained all manner of minnows, chubs, frogs, crayfish, water bugs, and an occasional water snake. We splashed among them all. We had no bathing suits, as such, but wore cutoff jeans that had worn through the first—or even second—generation of knee patches, and the bottoms hacked off.

The hole itself was not much larger around than a good sized hot tub, and just one or two strokes of what passed for us as swimming took you from one side to the other. We even fished in it. An occasional four or five inch chub would grab one of our hooked worms.

Additional delights were to be found along other stretches. When there was a fair volume of water running, we floated all manner of things downstream: cans, bottles, crude homemade boats, then, bombarded them with rocks. Ultimately, we would upgrade our arsenal to BB guns. These were the war years, and our targets were German or Japanese vessels, to be attacked from our shore batteries and sunk, before they bobbed out of range of our cannonade.

In the spring, the rains and snow melt would turn the crick into a fearsome torrent. We ventured down to watch it, and could hear large rocks being tumbled end over end by the force of the current. At these times, the crick was far from the gentle brook that would provide us with so much fun later. It seemed dangerous and threatening, and we kept our distance.

During the heat of a long summer, the stream was often reduced to a sluggish trickle. Pools would shrink and some disappear. This would reveal new wonders. Areas that had been scoured by the spring floods would have moved the channel a bit to one side or another. We would see new sand bars and pockets of gravel previously unknown. We would explore these endlessly, looking for the gold that we knew must be there. We never found any, but, now and then, as we wandered along the stream bed, we would come upon something intriguing—half buried in the sand. What in the world...? We would commence to dig.

It might be an old plow point, the tine from a harrow, a sheet of tin—perhaps blown from a barn roof—other metal objects the origin of which we couldn't identify. It was all salvaged and laid away to await the next visit of the scrap man.

During the war years, parents—ours included—were genuinely terrified of the dreaded Infantile Paralysis—Polio. The disease and its means of infection didn't seem to be well understood. Certain food items were associated with the affliction and were removed from our diet. I remember that peaches were one of the suspect fruits, and I don't believe I was allowed one during those years. Turnips—which I could as well have done without—apparently passed the health muster, and I was permitted any number of them.

I am amazed, as I think back on it now, that the crick was not put off limits to us. By the end of summer we would be covered with stings, welts, cuts, bug bites, scratches—badges from our summer fun—and all bathed in the crick. It drained the woods, fields and pastures to the north and east of our farm.

It carried the flotsam of the farms and wilds it traversed. it was a watering hole for every critter known to those parts, and carried God knows what with it. But it also carried the joys of our boyhood. Perhaps in the great wisdom of nature, it also carried our immunization.

Epilogue: Many years after these events, a granddaughter entered the family. Pettite, brown-eyed, adventurous—in the mold of her mother. A crick ran behind her house. She looked down on it as a babe in arms, and as a toddler, visited it holding the hand of a parent or older sibling. Its draw, though, was immediate. Soon enough, she was on her own and free to roam up and down this stream of wonders.

Her discoveries were manifold. Fishes and frogs, crawfish and polliwogs. Strange and wonderful stones and bits of flotsom.

Like the crick of my boyhood, it trickled benignly and presented a new and different adventure every day. If she turned up late for a meal or could not be found in her room, it became a given that "Ashley is down playing in the crick again!"

The Fireball Eight

Getting your first automobile is usually such a momentous occasion that you rarely consider that it will likely be just the first of many you will own in your lifetime. It is a consuming passion until it is replaced—after some longer or shorter period—and you begin to realize that cars are commodities, like clothes and shoes. Replacements will be needed from time to time.

I once heard it said that when men were asked about the best car they ever owned, they made the judgment based not on reliability or efficiency or performance, but chose the car they had the most fun with.

No contest in my case. Shortly after high school, I got a decent job, and bought a used 1949 Buick Super 2-door fastback sedanette—fire engine red. Ah me.

The engine was Buick's "Fireball 8," a straight 8 engine that generated a whopping 120 horsepower or so. This was actually not too bad for the day.

It wasn't until 1955 that the Chrysler 300—for 300 horsepower—came out, then several years after that, when the muscle cars made 120 seem downright anemic. Even if it had had a bigger mill, though, you couldn't have done much with the Dynaflow transmission—"dynaslush" to the stick shift boys who snickered at your big red land yacht. Performance wise, the Fireball 8 was no ball of fire.

Let them snicker. Buick was not really interested in the hot rod set. The Fireball wallowed in the corners, and had the turning radius of the Queen Mary. You could almost hear the long straight eight engine sucking raw gas through the carburetor to push the pistons, that would spin the turbines in the transmission—until the fluid achieved enough viscous inertia (or whatever the physics involved would be called) to move this barge from 0 to 60 MPH—in a mile or so. It took longer in cold weather, when the fluid was thicker. Eventually, though, you were up to speed and cruising along in style. Looks, size and luxury trumped all the horsepower and handling stuff in this machine. You could spread out a picnic on the hood.

Buick, at that time, was the midrange General Motors offering. It was the car for those who had moved up from the Chevys and Pontiacs but weren't quite ready for the Caddy— and the Super was the midrange of the Buicks.

It had three portholes on each front fender. This made it immediately distinguishable—in my view—from the tacky two porthole Special and the overly ostentatious four porthole Roadmaster models. Three seemed just right to me.

The Buick portholes came out of an idea by Ned Nickles, Buick's styling chief at the time. He drove a Roadmaster and had four amber lights installed on each side of the hood. He attached them to the engine's distributor. They flashed on and off as the cylinders fired and were meant to simulate the flames from the exhaust stacks of a World War II fighter plane. Coupled with the car's iconic "bombsight" hood ornament, it gave the driver the sense that he was at the controls of an imaginary fighter. The joke was that the bombsight made it easier to line up on pedestrians caught on the crosswalk between traffic light changes. In 1949, the portholes were added to all Buick models—less the flashing lights, of course.

Ok, it's the mid 1950's and it's a Saturday. That morning you washed and waxed your pride and joy to within an inch of its enameled hide. You applied a cleaner to the white wall tires (did I mention them?) and some chrome polish until you could see your face in the hubcaps. Once those jobs are done, you reinstalled the fender skirts and the "curb feelers."

Now it's early evening, and you pull the Fireball up in front of your girlfriend's house You have an air freshener hanging off the rear view mirror and your "suicide knob" installed on the steering wheel—the better to give you some steering leverage for the one-armed driving you will be doing in just a bit. Your steady, by the way, is a redhead. How's that for color coordination? She meets you at the door, and you escort her to your wheels. She sits at a discreet distance away on the pew-sized front seat and off you go. You are dying to close the distance. The suicide knob will not be put into play, though, until you are down the street and have turned the corner off her block, hiding your maneuvers from anyone watching your departure from her house. No fool, you.

Give those old cast iron blocks their due. No high rev Japanese whine from those babies. You get a nice mellow purr from your glass pack muffler. Absent any seatbelt, your date slides over next to you and you get a whiff of her perfume. White Shoulders is a current favorite. It doesn't seem to conflict much with your Pine air freshener and you find the combo of forest and floral strangely energizing.

You stop by to pick up Bruce and Sally—your double date companions for the evening. They settle down in the back seat of the Super—a space larger than some small kitchens of the period. You can vouch for this, having spent a little time in this area yourself. You check your rear view mirror, and notice that most of this space seems wasted—at least for the time being—since your friends are occupying just one small corner of it, as the four of you cruise to the drive-in.

Once there, you get your soft drinks, popcorn, hang the speaker on the driver's side window and settle in. A "creature feature" is playing and that means there will be plenty of opportunities for your girl to snuggle up closer as the onscreen heroine is harassed by some outer space slime ball. You notice that the windows of cars all around you are steamed up. You are a bit damp yourself.

I'll spare you all of the evening details—this is about the automobile, after all. Let me just say that your car—safely and comfortably—fulfills its dately duties. You all agree the movie was great, but don't recall many of the details. You drop your double date companions off to make their curfews, and then head for your girlfriend's house to make sure she gets home under the wire.

Not before idling the big boat over to the curb about a block from her house and sliding her toward you across the two yards of aqua-silver speckled broadcloth front seat. You exchange one last toe curling kiss and then you pull around the corner and walk her to her front door, where you exchange a chaste peck for the benefit of her parents and older brother, who are sure to be at some window checking for such stuff under the porch light.

It's a nice summer night. The Fireball Eight is purring along. You have the window cranked down and some AM station is playing the Four Aces "Love Is A Many Splendored Thing." Ain't that the truth. You wouldn't trade this set of wheels for any you can think of.

You know for sure that you are going to have to stop under a nearby street light and check for lipstick smudges before you pull into your own driveway. The old man will likely be up late watching "Greatest Fights of the Century" on the TV. He will have cracked a Pabst or three and will be mellow enough to offer you one. This will kill the taste of the last kiss, which you have been savoring—but you know there will be more.

Physicists say that matter and energy slide back and forth across a continuum—nothing is ever really destroyed. "Nature doesn't know extinction," Von Braun once famously said; "all it knows is transformation." Exactly. So it's out there somewhere on the planet. It could be a pile of rust oxidizing in some scrapyard, or recycled and part of some kid's matchbox car—elements of it exist somewhere.

Some enthusiast might even have restored it—a genuine reclaimed 1949 Buick Super 2-door fastback Fireball 8 sedanette—fire engine red. Imagine that!

If we get our choice of heavenly chariot transport, I want them to send that one for me. I'll drive. Need a lift?

Chuck Thurston

About the author

Chuck Thurston is one of five brothers raised on a small farm in Pennsylvania. He served in the United States Coast Guard, and flew in search and rescue seaplanes. He spent over 30 years at IBM.

In earlier days, in between times, and in later years he has been: a turret lathe operator in a factory; a newspaper reporter and columnist; a pick and shovel grunt for a landscaping company; an instructor for North Carolina State University in their Industrial Extension Service

He has a BS from Elmira (NY) College, and graduate degrees from SUNY Geneseo and Appalachian State University. He is married to Heidi Wibroe Thurston from Copenhagen, Denmark. The couple lives in Kannapolis, North Carolina. Their three children are grown with families of their own, and have contributed seven grandchildren—and two greats—to the mix.

He has published columns, editorials and essays in many newspapers and periodicals.

Senior Scribbles Second Dose *is his second book in this series. His first—*Senior Scribbles Unearthed *is available on Amazon.*

Chuck Thurston

CPSIA information can be obtained at www.ICGtesting.com
Printed in the USA
LVOW10s2348300114

371752LV00016B/304/P